Some Days are Diamonds
Some are Prune Pits

Musings of a Writer

by
LaVerna O'Neill Conrad

3DW Press

Some Days are Diamonds Some are Prune Pits: Musings of a Writer

Cover and Interior Design - Anna Goldsworthy

Printed in the United States by 3DW Press
ISBN-13: 978-0692947562 (3DW Press)
ISBN-10: 0692947566

First Printing, 2017

Also by LaVerna J. Conrad:

A Beginning Book for Aspiring Writers: A Guide for Anyone Wanting to Write for Publication

Praise for
Some Days Are Diamonds
Some are Prune Pits

LaVerna, I am so touched by today's blog blessing the men in your life. What a beautiful expression of recognition and appreciation. Knowing the wholeness that is you, I'm pretty sure they're not doing it for your husband -- they're doing it for you!

I continue to be inspired by your dedication, focus, and talent as a writer.

--Nina Durfee, Author and Editor
NinaDurfee.com

I love what you do with the every day occurring events!

--Dale W.

LaVerna's blog about high maintenance traveling made me laugh out loud. It reminded me of my Mom's light green suitcase (without wheels...do they still make suitcases without wheels?) She brings it everywhere she goes. Between her and Dad I often wonder if there is anything in it other than medical equipment and medication.

Her article also reminded me of ME. I suspect I have pills in my purse that expired while Clinton was in office.

--Diane G., Executive Coach

Finally got a chance to read your story. What a winter adventure - and today, since I'm snowed in, was the perfect day to read it. I especially liked the part about Santa and the spirit of Christmas. I hope you keep writing more of your story. Stay warm and safe!

-- Joyce KM, Teacher

Dedication

This book is dedicated to Anna Marie Goldsworthy. Without her help and encouragement this book would never have been written.

Table of Contents

Lessons Life Has Taught Me

Chapter 1

We start learning from the day we are born. After a bit we find out that if we cry we'll be fed or changed and it goes on.

I learned in first grade that something I did made someone else cry. I thought it was really funny to take my crayon and scribble on the paper of the boy in front of me. What I thought was funny was not and had consequences. When he came back from the reading group and found out what I had done, he didn't laugh, he cried and the teacher made me stand in the corner.

Then there was the time my sister was brought home from the hospital after having had her appendix removed. People brought her gifts including a bowl of fruit. I thought I should be a help to her and serve the fruit to her visitors. I was wrong there too and another lesson learned.

Donald Larberg and his friend taught me how to invent excuses. They were bullies and they scared me into running away from them. For days they tortured me by chasing me almost home. I guess they didn't chase me all the way because they didn't want to be caught. As a result of this, I made up all kinds of reasons to leave school early to avoid them. They always managed to catch up anyway.

Mrs. Yerion, my teacher, caught on to what was happening and took care of it. She just kept them after school and that gave me plenty of time to get home.

The learning kept coming. Miss Cass, our science teacher, taught a class on human reproduction including showing us a fetus preserved in a jar. This class included both boys and girls. Talk about embarrassing and gross. That one tops the list. Even so it was a lesson learned.

Embarrassing or not, no matter how old one gets the learning goes on. Take that from one who has lived long enough to know.

Sept. 30, 2017

All About "the Talk"

Chapter 2

You have to go through it sooner or later, so you might just as well resign yourself to it. Get prepared with your answers to the questions you know will be asked, and also be prepared for those (out of the blue) that get dropped on you. Just because you're over 85, don't think they'll go easy on you. Oh no. They want to know all your business, and they'll find out, too. Medicare wants to know, and that makes it official.

The first question I was asked was, "Are you depressed?" I don't think so. How do you tell if you're depressed anyway? If you were, couldn't they just tell by looking at you? Would you have a "hang dog" look with droopy eyes or something telltale like sloping shoulders and hanging head? I didn't have any of these things, so I gave them a no.

Other questions answered, it was on to the clock face. Gee, it was back to first grade. Boy, that was a no-brainer. 12, 6, 3, 9 and put the hands wherever they want them.

There were questions about scatter rugs, grab bars in the bathroom, and, "Have you talked with your attorney?" "Do you have voluntary end-of-life planning?" Well, it is kind of hard to plan when you don't know when you're going.

By that time my patience was at an end. You'll have to watch that. When she asked for three words, I indignantly came out with OH MY GOODNESS! Then, realizing, they were three words, I let them stand.

You will get results through the mail, or at least I did. Then go through them and find out that regardless of aches and pains, we're pretty darn normal....

Mon, Feb 06, 2012

Job Hunting Strategies

Chapter 3

According to the National Writer's Club publication, Lynette Dryer Vuong worked and waited for fourteen years to get her book published. She submitted it 44 times, sent out 76 query letters, and rewrote the book three times before it was finally published.

Meg Hill wrote in the Writer's Digest that she had submitted her story 124 times before it finally sold. It was bought by a magazine that had rejected it twice before.

Helen J. Anderson started out writing about what she knew. She sent out articles typical of the housewife and mother she was. After a year of rejections and being told to give up because of the considerable competition she was facing, she came up with a new thought. One must not only write about what one knows, but it also has to be something that other people don't know about. Working from this angle, she started over again, and in the next 18 months she sold 16 articles.

Persistence pays off, not only in writing but in job hunting. If you are looking for a job, remember the persistence of these people and hang in there. Maybe the very next place you go will have an opening for you. Or maybe you need to stop and rethink, like Helen J. Anderson, and approach the problem from a different angle. Jobs are out there. The competition is terrific and jobs are fewer, but believe in yourself and your abilities, pray for guidance, and be persistent in searching.

You may be surprised like my father was during the Great Depression. He had a family to support and was out of work. He made a list of possible places that might be hiring. On the top of his list was the Washington Grade School in Auburn. Construction was to start the next Monday morning, so he got up early on that day and went to the site. There was only one person there sitting on a log. Father, thinking this man was also looking for work, sat down beside him and began to talk to him. They talked for quite a while until a third man drove up in a truck. Hopping out, he asked the first man,"Hired anyone yet?"

"Just this man," said the man on the log, and he pointed to my father.

It had been so easy. All it took was knowing what was going on in the community and getting there early.

More on this next time....

Feb 16, 2012

Job Hunting Strategies - Part 2

Chapter 4

Reading the paper gave my father the knowledge to be in the right place at the right time for a job. It wasn't the best job, but it provided enough money for food and allowed him to pay his bills.

In my experience, reading the newspaper also helped me find a job; but it was the Society Column that provided the clue. The Superintendent of the Sumner Schools, instead of advertising in the Classified section, sent a note to the editor that the secretary of the grade school was leaving. When I read that, I called his office and got an appointment for an interview that afternoon. I was hired on the spot, not as secretary to the grade school Principal, but as the Superintendent's secretary.

Keeping up on the news in your area is important. If a company is laying off 250 workers, it's probably a waste of time to apply there.

You have to keep yourself open to all possibilities for employment -- even to being your own boss. In 1932, my father had just this kind of chance. He heard about a milk route that was up for grabs. Even though the last man that had it went bankrupt, my father decided to go for it anyway.

The next day he went to the Medosweet Dairies in Tacoma to check it out. They told him if he had a truck there the next day, he could have the route. He had no truck but told them he would be there with a truck. His next problem was to get one, so he went to Scarff Motors in Auburn, talked to the owner, and got his truck.

I don't know how he worked that, but I suppose that Mr. Scarff wasn't selling many trucks anyway, so took a chance on him.

The milk shippers had concerns and one asked him, "Are you going to charge us less than that last guy?"

"No, I'll charge you more. But I'll do more for you when you need help."

My father not only made that milk route pay, he increased it to the point where he added another truck and gave another guy a job.

So, when the economy is bad and you need to support yourself, don't just look for jobs, look for opportunities, and don't be afraid to take a chance. Read your newspaper or papers and find out what is happening in your area, and don't give up. Like the writers, be persistent. Be innovative. Talk to people. Network. Jobs are out there, and you only need one.

Good Luck and Happy Hunting!!

Feb 23, 2012

Constructive Apprehension

Chapter 5

The interviewer asked John Glenn if he was afraid when he took off in the capsule for his first ride into space. Glenn laughed and said it wasn't fear, but more like constructive apprehension. That started me thinking. I had never heard that term before. All the other ways to say you are, or were, afraid came to mind. Having the willies, the creeps, butterflies in the stomach, the heebie jeebies, the jitters, cold feet, fear and trembling, or shaking in your boots. Scared, frightened, dreading, fearfulness, terror, horror, or alarm. Probably a lot more terms express the feeling.

My father weighed in on fear when he teased my mother about her fear of snakes. He said she was very religious because every time she saw a snake she called upon her Maker (that was the only time Mother swore).

Through the years, people are quoted as speaking on the subject. Burke, for one, had this to say. "Early and provident fear is the mother of safety." Even Shakespeare said. "Present fears are less than horrible imaginings."

The quote I like best is from H. W. Beecher, who said, "God planted fear in the soul as truly as he planted hope or courage.... It is a kind of bell or gong which rings the mind into quick life and avoidance on the approach of danger.... It is the soul's signal for rallying."

That bell, or gong, has gone off in my life many times and saved me, especially while driving the car. There are times I have slammed on the brakes to avoid hitting a car that suddenly turned in front of me or did some other maneuver that would have caused a collision. Also many times I moved past my fears and did things I was afraid to do, and all went well. In fact, I feel I became stronger by facing my fears. But, there were other times when my fears made me change my plans or change my route. Was I saved from disaster at those times? I will probably never know. It's because we'll never know about these things that we'd best pay attention to our fears - just in case.

Take care and be constructive in your apprehensions!

Mar 01, 2012

Kudos to Louise

Chapter 6

My neighbor Louise has struck a blow for all of us and shown us the way. We have been driven to distraction by "robo" calls. Especially, "Card Member Services, this is Rachel". When the calls come, it is always three in a day, and the days come often.

When I first began to get them, I would immediately hang up on "Rachel" and then call the 800 # for my card member service to see if anything was wrong with my account. After a few months of this, they told me that the only times they would call was when something was wrong. It would be the legal department if someone was misusing the account. If there was something wrong with a payment, it would be the accounting department. They would identify themselves by giving the real name of the company, the department and the reason for calling. Their real name is not Card Member Services, even though that's the name you use when you pay them.

This whole thing became so irritating. However, not thinking past the irritation, I just kept on hanging up on "Rachel". Louise, on the other hand, decided to do something. She listened to the message and when it said, "If you want to know more, punch this number," she punched it. Lo and behold, she got a real person. Let me tell you, that person got an earful. All that pent-up emotion came forth and Louise let him have it. I don't think "Rachel" will call her anytime soon.

I'm now waiting for "Rachel" to be working this area again. I'm saving up words and phrases to let them know, in no uncertain terms, that if they call me again, I'll sue.

Mar 07, 2012

A Boost to Morale

Chapter 7

Today I called my son and his wife to see if they were all right. I'd heard from my granddaughter that her folks hadn't been to church on Sunday so I had to check. They were fine, just had a problem with the time change. However, my son and I talked for over an hour. That fact made me change my plans for the day. Instead of going shopping, I'd go to my local Rite Aid and buy just the things I was out of.

When I went to leave the store, a man was coming in. He was leaning heavily on a cane, and I didn't recognize him. He brightened when he saw me, though, and started talking. Then I remembered him, even though I hadn't seen him in a long time. In fact, I thought he had passed away, but since I never knew his name, I couldn't be sure. Now, here he was. He was always hanging out at either Rite Aid or the gas station. I had seen him several times in the past, at one or the other of these places. He always talked to me, always joking. In fact, one time when he knew I was going to the gas station after Rite Aid, he hurried over there. When I drove up, he opened the door and said. "What kept you?"

Before I left the gas station that day, I told him I was going to Costco next and he better not be there, or there would be trouble. Since he was a joker, not a stalker, he didn't carry it any further.

Today was such a bad day. The wind brought down several new branches that will stay until Bob, my yard maintenance guy, comes and cleans them up. Then there's the rain. It's depressing. Therefore, to meet this funny man (who tried to get me to invite him to dinner at my house, and when that didn't work, invited me to his place) was definitely a depression breaker. No doubt if I'd taken him up on any of his proposals, he wouldn't have known what to do. He probably doesn't have many women who will pay attention to him anymore. But let me tell you, at my age to get hit on, even in fun, is a real morale booster.

Mar 14, 2012

Home Remedies of the Thirties

Chapter 8

Whenever Mother thought we were exposed to some disease, we got a dose of Castor Oil. She would give it to us with orange juice, which did not mitigate the taste and only succeeded in our disliking orange juice as well. It probably did not help all that much, because we still had mumps, measles, chicken pox, and even scarlet fever -- all those diseases that were around when we were growing up.

I remember we had to gargle our sore throats with Extol (a McKesson product) that we thought was yucky. It did have a pretty pink color though. We also had to take Jayne's Vermifuge for intestinal worms. This was a medicine that really tasted good. Since it tasted so good, I now doubt its ability to be of any value and question if we really needed it anyway.

Another thing mother used was Mustang Liniment for earaches. It was daubed on the outer ear canal and amazingly made our earaches better. Whether they were going to get better by themselves or whether the liniment helped will never be known.

Epsom Salts were used to draw out the poison when there was an infection, or the possibility of one. One summer when

I was running around barefoot, I stepped on a rusty nail. Right away mother got out the basin, filled it with warm water, and added Epsom Salts. I soaked my foot in it for the time Mother thought was right, and then she put some of the crystals on a wet cloth and bandaged my foot with it. As far as I can remember, I never had a tetanus shot, and my foot healed fine.

Mentholatum was used for scrapes, cuts, and scratches and had an amazing healing quality. It was also put on your chest when you had a cold. It did make you breathe better. Whether it attacked the cause or not is open to question.

With all the talk about our antibiotics being overused and probably producing super germs that we won't be able to deal with, maybe we should look into those old remedies that people used, and see what they really can do.

Mar 22, 2012

Junk Rooms and Longevity

Chapter 9

Do you have a junk room? Most people have at least a junk drawer where all nondescript stuff goes. As a last resort, you look into it for your car keys or whatever other small item you haven't been able to find. Ten to one it isn't there either.

Well, I have a junk room, and my son has seen it. His response to my junk room: "Mother, you are not going to your reward until you clean that room. We're not going to do it."

Okay, so I'll clean it. But. And that's the problem, a big however here. How can you get rid of these things that you might need some time in the future? All that wrapping paper saved from past parties surely can be used again. Of course, you have to have ribbon to go with the wrapping, so you save that too. Then there are those scraps of carpeting that might be needed to patch a hole somewhere. Not to mention those boxes of scrap material that can be used to make a quilt (when I get around to it). Let's not forget all those old Christmas decorations that my children made. How can I part with those? Then there's that folding bed my friend gave me. How could I say no (even though I have another one downstairs). And how about those other treasures that I've found at thrift stores? Just because I haven't found a use for them yet doesn't necessarily mean I won't.

So, what to do about this? One thing comes to mind: keeping my junk room a junk room, since I can't go to my reward until it's gone, should ensure my longevity. Wouldn't you say?

Mar 29, 2012

Mistakes and Learnings

Chapter 10

"Experience teaches you one thing: You've made another mistake." The entrance to the left turn lane had been lengthened by a couple of car lengths. Not knowing this, I went to my usual turn place and turned, thinking that's where I was supposed to turn. I went up the ramp, got on the freeway, and then I heard the siren and pulled over. I remember asking the officer if he was sure he wanted me. "Oh yes," he said. "I could have hit you broadside. You turned right in front of me". Then he gave me the ticket. Later when I told my father about it, he wisely told me that you should never think you have to turn at a certain place. If you're not sure about the exit, go around the block and take another look at it. Be sure you're right before you make your move.

That advice is good with a phone too. We had a phone with numbers programmed in. Then all we had to do was punch a button and that number would be automatically dialed. The first button was for 911, the second was for our next-door neighbors, and so on. I was sitting on the couch and reached over to call our neighbors and hit the first button instead of the second. "911. What is your emergency?" Oh shoot, I didn't want them, so I hung up and carefully hit the second button. I was busily engaged talking to my neighbor, when there was a knock on the door, and someone was opening the door and coming in. What do you say to a policeman in the performance of his duty? "Gee, thanks for stopping by," didn't seem to cut it. I had to promise next time (and he was sure there would be a next time) I would stay on the line and tell them I'd goofed up.

Talking about goofing up, I did that big time with spray paint. Do you know that spray cans are under pressure? That is how they can spray paint where you aim. One of my recent lessons was just that. It's a lesson you don't want to forget. It can cause you no end of trouble. I hired a guy that was out of work to sand and paint my railings. My son had bought the cans of spray paint some time ago but hadn't had time to do the job. So, I thought this was the best solution. It'll give this man some gas money and get the cans off the porch. A good idea, except for one thing: those cans had sat there for a long time, and one can got plugged. The guy (I'd use the man's name here, but I'm sure he wants to remain nameless), took off the cap. When it wouldn't spray, he took off the button and brought it in the house to see if I could unplug it. Why of course I could. He went back out to work, and I went to get a sharp object. With a needle in hand and the can on the kitchen table, I went to work. The minute I stuck that needle in the top of that can it was like Mt. Vesuvius erupting. I couldn't get the can out the door fast enough. Paint splattered on ceiling, table, bench, walls, floor, door, porch, and me. Suddenly, the guy remembered he had to leave. Another job down the road was waiting for him. This spring, you know what I'll be doing. It's suddenly time to repaint the kitchen.

Apr 05, 2012

What's in a Name?

Chapter 11

"That which we call a rose by any other name would smell as sweet."

When one of my friends, who was in a hurry and saying hello to a group of us, couldn't remember my name and called me Whatchamacallit, some of the ladies gasped, but I laughed. I've been guilty many times of forgetting someone's name, so how could I be upset with someone who had a lapse of memory, especially when she's such a funny and loving person who means no harm to anyone? It's not what you're called, but how it's meant that counts.

I have been called the sheep lady, the apple lady and probably other names I don't know about that aren't complimentary. (If I ever cut you off in traffic, I'm sorry).

Today when I went to pick up my friend, I found her neighbor, Jackie, who does her yard work. When Jackie saw me, she asked. "Are you the letter writer?" My friend immediately introduced us, so now she knew my name and went off to get her husband. Her husband, Bob Whalen, has been a council member in Milton for some time. He immediately quit what he was working on and came over to meet me. Shaking my hand, he thanked ME for what I've done for the city. I was shocked. I should be thanking him instead. He's the one that goes Monday after Monday to meetings and fights the battles that make our city a better place to live. All I've done is publish a couple of letters to the editor in our local paper. Since I had no feedback on those letters, I thought no one read them. Now I know at least the Milton City Council read them. So now people can call me the letter writer lady, and if they can't think of that, Whatchamacallit will do.

Apr 12, 2012

The Way
of Policy Changes

Chapter 12

On the way to the escalator of our largest and most impressive department store, my daughter and I came upon the following scene.

A mother and her small son were strolling along when the mother spotted a sale table off to her right and stopped to examine its contents. While she was busily engaged, the child wandered over to the other side of the aisle into a floor display of a complete nursery. It was so complete and homelike that the boy, whom we judged to be about three, finding nature's call upon him, proceeded to use these so handily set-up facilities. The mother remained unaware, as did the busy clerks. We decided since it was too late already, who were we to tell them? We proceeded to the escalator.

We couldn't help but think, though, that one small boy, in his innocence, was busily engaged in changing policy in the display department.

Apr 19, 2012

Children's Abilities

Chapter 13

Two middle school boys in our town were touted as heroes because they stopped a school bus and gave aid to the stricken driver. All twelve on the bus were remarkable. Though they were obviously scared, they didn't panic or scream. You could hear some say, "Call 911." Someone else said, "Turn off the key." They were all thinking about what needed to be done. The boy that steered the bus turned off the key so the bus rolled to a stop, and catastrophe was averted.

This is a remarkable story, but maybe not unique. I would say never underestimate the ability of children. For example: Jeff Jaschke, of Randall, Minnesota, saved his father's life. He and his two-year-old brother were sitting in a wagon watching their father unloading corn, when the father's hand got caught in the corn-picking machine. Within minutes, Jeff ran to the tractor and brought it and the power take-off to a halt, preventing his father from being pulled into the machine. He then ran to the house to get his mother, who called neighbors to come and help. By the time they got there, Jeff had brought out tools and wrenches to loosen the rollers to get his father's hand out. Unbelievable for a four-year-old, yet he watched his father all the time, evidently absorbing information and obviously learning from it.

Then there is Jimmy Roland from Shawnee, Oklahoma, who, at age six, saved his family. They lived out in the country. When his mother heard a noise, she took a pan and went out to investigate, telling the children to get the gun. When she got outside, a man grabbed her and put a knife against her throat. Jimmy came to his mother's rescue with the gun and told the man to let his Momma go, or he'd shoot. The man told Jimmy to put the weapon down, but instead Jimmy cocked the gun, which made the man loosen his grip enough so Jimmy's mother was able to free herself. Jimmy scared the guy (and his two friends) with a gun that wasn't even loaded. He said he hadn't had time to hunt for the shells. His big brother taught him how to shoot, but his father didn't allow loaded guns in the house, and the shells were hidden.

Brian Hurley of Port Orchard, Washington, saved his sister from drowning in a baby sitters pool when he was seven. His sister was floating around the pool on a big ball, then slid off, began floundering, and disappeared beneath the surface. The baby sitter had left the children alone for a few minutes. Jennifer, nine years old, ran to get the baby sitter, but Brian thought about it for half a second and then jumped in to save his little sister. He found her on the bottom, grabbed hold of her arm, and pulled her to the surface. When Jennifer came back with the baby sitter, Brian had four-year-old Jackie out of the pool. He had been able to do this because he had taken lessons at a pool in Purdy, though he was quoted as saying, "I don't like to swim."

So, kids are still kids, and we don't know what they are capable of until life puts them to the test.

Apr 26, 2012

Waiting for the Coroner

Chapter 14

It was a cold, dark night in November, the blowing wind adding to the misery of the constantly falling rain. Emergency vehicles sat with their diesel engines rhythmically sounding off, while their staff cleaned up the equipment and got ready for whatever was coming next. When everything was in order, the drivers began to move their vehicles. Leaving one by one, the two fire trucks and three EMT trucks drove quietly away. They had done all they could, but it was not enough to bring back the man we now must guard; the body they left lying on the blacktop covered with a sheet.

Back at the station, some officers were commenting to my friend who had come with me to go on a ride-a-long with the police. "She's going to have a hard time dealing with this," they said. My friend Dusty knows me pretty well, I guess, because she just laughed and said, "Oh, you don't know Mrs. C. She'll deal with it, all right." And I guess I did.

After the last diesel drove away, there was silence. Except for the rain and wind, we heard nothing. It was eerie. The officer wasn't saying anything, so I thought I'd better talk. There was no telling how long we'd have to wait. My writing mind came to the forefront, and I decided to find out what I could about this deceased man. Although I would never know his name, I did find out he had done some shopping at Safeway and then gone to his truck in the upper part of the parking lot. Someone realized he was having trouble, and they rushed into Safeway and told a clerk to call 911. That's how it started. I then decided I should get a picture. At first the officer was upset with that idea, but he soon relented when he realized all I would get would be a picture of a white mound.

It was hard to carry on a conversation with the officer. He seemed to be having more difficulty dealing with this than I was. Finally, the coroner's van arrived with only one man. The officer helped him put the body on the gurney and transport it to the van, but as they were moving the gurney, a leg slid off and dangled there. Both men were disturbed by this and carefully placed the leg back on the gurney. They showed a reverence for that body, and I'm sure not just because I was watching, but because they were good people. In checking the man's wallet, they found he had an apartment nearby, and they would go there to find next of kin. Since I was not allowed to go with them, I would have to wait in the police car. The officer assured me I would be safe in the locked car, and he drove to a dark street nearest the deceased's apartment. There he left me to spend the rest of the night watching through the rain-soaked window at the traffic light on the corner changing from red to green and green to red.

May 03, 2012

Fingerprints in the Butter

Chapter 15

As a mother, one of the hardest decisions I had to make when we were going out with the family was whether I got the kids ready first or myself ready first. It was one of those things where you couldn't win no matter which way you went. With four children aged 5 years and under, if you got them ready first, one was bound to find something to get into that was messy. If I got ready first, the baby would no doubt spit up on me. With four little ones, I was too busy to spend time trying to figure it out. So I didn't think about it anymore, just plunged in and hoped for the best.

As time passed, things seemed to improve in that department, so we invited my husband's boss and his wife over for dinner. That day the weather was nice, so I sent the yard children outside to play in the sandbox, put the baby in her crib, and started cooking. While things were cooking, I set the table and checked the outside kids to make sure they weren't killing each other and that no neighbor kids had invaded the yard.

When my husband got home from work, he got ready and then spelled me off with the kids so I could get ready. Everything was going according to plan. I then took over with the little ones, and at the very last minute we brought in the yard children to scrub off the dirt and put them in clean clothes for company.

With all ready and looking great, the company came, and husband and I went to greet them. While my husband took coats and made our guests comfortable, I got the kids lined up to greet them. Their little faces were beaming, their hands were so clean, and not a spot was on their clothes anywhere. I felt so proud of myself. Now it was time to bring everyone to the table.

We were all seated and enjoying the meal when I noticed the butter -- but too late to whisk it off the table. Everyone had seen it. Someone had decided to taste the butter before dinner and left little holes and fingerprints in it. Our guests were too polite to mention it, I suppose, and I couldn't think of anything to say that would help. So, nothing was said or done. I just sat there quietly thinking I love my children very much, but this being a mother is a humbling experience.

May 10, 2012

It's National Police Week

Chapter 16

In honor of them, I would like to repeat something that was printed in the News Tribune some years ago about a fallen officer. Officer Nollmeyer was killed in the line of duty by a murderer he was pursuing in a Tacoma alley.

"Like his law enforcement colleagues, Patrolman Craig A. Nollmeyer was a human extension of the law, a part of the living shield that enables us to go about our daily lives in reasonable order and safety. The tragedy that struck Nollmeyer so swiftly reminds us how dependent we are on that shield, and how much we owe to the daily courage of those in Nollmeyer's profession."

In the performance of their duties, law enforcement people suffer stress, minor injuries, sometimes major injuries, their family life is continually disrupted, and, yes, sometimes they die.

Policemen are in a war that never ends. They are not supermen, nor do they walk on water; but they are super human beings trying hard to do a good job. Craig Nollmeyer's widow said at his funeral, "It doesn't make the hurt any less... but, there is a purpose in it. Craig died defending a system he believed in."

Give the law enforcement officers in your area your full support. They deserve no less.

May 17, 2012

A Memorial Day Tribute

Chapter 17

When Ollie Gove discovered that the Spanish American War veterans were not being taken care of, she did something about it. She helped those she could by writing letters to their families and then got busy and made their plight known.

She started a Women's Relief Corp group in Auburn with some of her friends, and every year from then on they helped celebrate Memorial Day in honor of our veterans.

There were assemblies in the schools where a prayer was said along with tributes to the soldiers, sailors, and marines who fought to keep our nation free. I remember going to one of these assemblies at the high school when I was in grade school. It was a very solemn but meaningful occasion, with all the children and some of the parents present.

There were also tributes at the Auburn Park where there was a cannon displayed. Sometimes Ollie Gove gave speeches at these events. She was always there in a leading capacity. So, on this Memorial Day I would like to thank the veterans for all they've done for our country and especially to show my appreciation for my grandmother, Olive Robertson Gove, for her part in keeping the memory of our veterans alive.

Note: Before Memorial Day each year, my family went to the cemetery to tend the graves of our loved ones, as did many others. While our parents cut the grass and trimmed around the headstones, we played. The Auburn Cemetery was a beautiful place, even then. It was always quiet and peaceful, so we were never afraid to be there. Then when Perpetual Care came in and our parents didn't have to go and do that job any more, we were kind of disappointed.

May 24, 2012

The News from My Neighborhood

Chapter 18

This morning I made the decision to put my dog, Rusty, to sleep. This was a hard decision to make. Our pets become so much a part of our lives that we find it really difficult to realize that they can't go all the way with us. We have to say goodbye to them long before others have to say goodbye to us. Rusty was obviously hurting: not eating anything, drinking a lot of water, and moving around a lot. Something else that concerned me was her left eye. It was slightly red and starting to protrude. I took her to a veterinary hospital.

The veterinarian was very nice and very good with Rusty. Before he saw her, money was discussed, and after he checked her out, I was told in order to go forward they would have to have the minimum deposit of $1275. Luckily, they take credit cards. At that time, the thing to do seemed to be to find out if she had cancer in that eye, which is what the doctor thought. I decided to leave her there overnight, and the next day they could take tests and determine the course of treatment.

I went to sleep thinking about what I should do and woke up with the answer, the right answer for Rusty. Simply put: she isn't hurting any more. Those intrusive tests and invasive surgeries won't be done, and the veterinarian agreed. It was just time to let her go.

Note: The other news in the neighborhood is this. I got nosey when I went out to put garbage in the can and saw my neighbors talking to a policeman. No longer having a dog to warn me of trouble, I thought I'd better find out what their problem was. She told me that the ornamental mailbox displayed by their driveway was blown up last night. Her husband had made it more than 20 years ago when he first retired. I had heard the blast and listened to the radio until I went to sleep, thinking that it had been a building that blew up and it would be reported on the news. I forgot all about the noise until she said the blast shook the house.

May 31, 2012

High Maintenance

Chapter 19

It takes a trip to make one realize she has come to the high maintenance stage. When you make your lists of what you need to take, it all becomes clear. You list your prescription pills, your over-the-counter pills, and your eye drops. Definitely don't forget your antacid, or you'll have heartburn that won't quit.

Then there's the make-up. Be sure and put in enough cover stick, or you'll scare people. Don't forget the powders and lotions. Then work on the clothes. Put in a good girdle, or foundation, as the ladies used to say. Remember, uplift is always good. Include an extra outfit or two, just in case you spill something and have to change. Be sure to add sweaters in case you get cold.

After you've made your lists, then go to the closet for that overnight bag. That's when you also realize you may only be staying overnight, but your requirements put you in the big suitcase category. No more overnight bags for you.

Of course, you need a big handbag as well. There are a few necessities that you carry with you at all times. The doctor is so fussy about a person carrying those heart pills, just in case. Since you have never used them, it might be a good plan to check them to see if they are still good, so add that to the preparation list. After that, high maintenance or not, just go on that trip and have a good time. I did that this last weekend.

Jun 07, 2012

Encouraging Words

Chapter 20

Life takes a lot of interesting turns, wouldn't you agree? At this time of people searching for jobs, trying to keep families fed and clothed, and just trying to hold their lives together, others have come up with things that help

It may be so simple that you say to yourself, "What can that do?"

One of the simplest things that I've come across is the pep talk in every drop put out by Hall's Cough Drops. If you had the symptoms of a head cold on top of today's worries, you would have a really depressing time. I was reminded of this last week when I came down with a virus (as my doctor told me). When your throat is sore, your head is stuffed up, your nose runs, your ears feel plugged and your eyes water, it may be caused by a virus. I call it a cold. You feel depressed and miserable. You gargle with warm salt water and get out an extra box of tissue, because you're going to need it. You drink lots of water, and when you cough, you get out those cough drops.

The nice surprise comes when you look at the wrapper that comes around the cough drop. It has words on it, encouraging words. You not only read them, you save them to read again. You feel better. You read: "Keep your chin up. Conquer today. Push on! Power through. Bet on yourself.

Hi-five yourself. March forward! Be unstoppable. Nothing you can't handle. Inspire envy. Tough is your middle name. Get back in there, champ. Don't waste a precious minute. You've survived tougher."

I don't know what effect these words have on you, but they reminded me that I have survived tougher. For this week, those words did a lot for me. I quit feeling sorry for myself and got some work done.

Jun 14, 2012

Is the World an Unfriendly Place?

Chapter 21

How do you view the world? What is your experience? Last week I was sick and had to go to the pharmacy to pick up a prescription that my doctor had ordered. It was not ready. I should have called first, but I didn't. That meant I'd have to go home and come back later or sit in their nice waiting room and wait. Since I felt so awful, all I wanted to do was sit down. Therefore, I went to the waiting room. It wasn't long before I was joined by a man who had to wait for his wife's prescription. We began to talk.

Funny how you feel better when you get your mind off yourself. This man was a retired longshoreman, and it wasn't long before I was hearing about the unfairness in some practices on the docks. I wish I had had a tape recorder with me, because I was hearing some really interesting stuff from a man who obviously knew what he was talking about. Stuff only an insider could tell you. With documentation, this could have made front-page news. I forgot about feeling so rotten and thought about others problems, and we went from the topic of his past work to the state of the country. On that we could agree a lot. This country, and the world, is in trouble. There we sat, two strangers from differing backgrounds, discussing the world's problems in a nice and civil manner. There was no way that he and I could change a thing. Talking about it helped, though. I hope he thought so, too. It just said to me that my world is still a friendly place, regardless of what's going on elsewhere.

Jun 21, 2012

It's All in the Attitude

Chapter 22

So many times I hear it's terrible to get old. People seem to dwell on what they can't do, rather than what they can do. To me, it's just another phase of life. And like Marion Anderson's mother, I just want to follow the road of life to see where it leads.

It lead me to the gas station Friday, where I met a man who came up to me and said, "You have beautiful hair. My wife has white hair like that. It started turning white when she was quite young."

I should have said thank you and let it go at that, but I didn't. I admitted it's not mine. I get it out of a box. I told him how I started wearing wigs. It was when I was substituting in the Federal Way School District. I'd get a call at 5:30 a.m. asking if I could come in that day. With a wig, of course I could. It didn't matter if I hadn't been able to get to the beauty shop to get my hair cut or taken care of; I was ready to go.

My great aunt, Aunty Ann, also wore a wig, though she called it a "transformation". When sulfa drugs first came out, Aunty Ann thought if a little does some good, a whole lot more would be better. She overdosed and lost all her hair. Those few that got to see her without her transformation told the rest of us that she was as bald as a billiard ball. Of course, those kids were held in high esteem by the rest of us cousins, because they were privileged having seen this sight.

The wig company I buy from says when you quit getting compliments on your hair, it's time to buy a new wig. I guess I can forget that for a while.

Jun 28, 2012

Road Rage

Chapter 23

Have you ever experienced it? If you have, you probably haven't forgotten it. I certainly haven't.

To some, people in my age group (from white hair on) are fair game. They think we can't fight back, so they witness against us, try us, and convict us in the court of no appeal.

My so-called infraction was cutting a guy off from a merging lane. I allowed a truck to go, then it was my turn. This guy was speeding to beat me out but I closed the gap and went on my way.

He followed me for two miles. I just thought it a coincidence that he was going the same way I was going When I turned to go behind the mall to go to the bank, I just thought he was going to the bank too.

I parked across the parking lot from the bank. He parked behind my car so I couldn't back out and started hollering at me. That's when I knew it was not innocent, it was deliberate. "You can hear me. You're a terrible driver. You shouldn't be allowed to drive, on and on." I thought, "He's just a hollerer. He won't hurt me." So, I got out to talk to him. In my side vision, I saw a woman leave her car and walk over to the bank. She was no help. She wasn't going to get involved.

There was no talking to this guy. He was there to punish me. That was it. When he got done, he backed straight out, still looking and hollering at me. If anyone had stepped out between the cars he would have hit them.

I stood in that parking lot and thought, "Am I that person he says I am, that terrible person who doesn't know how to drive and shouldn't be allowed to?" I didn't have to think about that very long. I wasn't that person. So, I went to the cash machine, got my money, and drove on to Auburn to go shopping.

Later I checked with the police chief, and he said I was in the right. Also, my lawyer said if I had gotten his license number so he could be identified, he could be arrested for illegal imprisonment.

Jul 05, 2012

The Men in My Life

Chapter 24

Did you notice? I'm using the plural here. Yes, there are men in my life. Most men who are brought up right tend to be Boy Scouts at heart. They are there when you need them.

Just last week, Bob (the guy who mows my lawn) started mowing by the garage first instead of the yard. He said by coincidence, but he was right there to carry a board out to the field that I needed for the sheep shearer who was coming that afternoon.

Leo is the sheep shearer who comes every year and does the job for me. Of course, I pay him, but I only have two sheep, and although it probably isn't cost effective, he does it and says he'll be back next year.

Then there's Jim who fixes things. He comes, no matter the weather, to fix the electricity or the leaks in the plumbing. He has shored up the floors, worked on the roof, and even readjusted my aerial so I could get my favorite channels.

I can't forget Pat and Mike, my Irish mechanics in Puyallup. I once had my left turn signal go out when I was in Sumner. I called them and they said, "Come on over. It's all right turns from Sumner." When my car got backed into, in a parking lot, they went online and found the part my old car needed and made it look like new again.

Dennis from next door drives a tour bus. He also belongs to a food co-op and brings me all kinds of bread to pass on to others. He happened to be bringing bread when he found out I was not able to turn on the outside water this spring. It didn't matter that he had his good clothes on. It was, "Where's your shovel?" I gave it to him, and within minutes he had fixed the problem and cleaned up the mess.

There's Bill, who gets sheep feed for me in the wintertime and always comes in to talk for a while, making those winter days brighter.

There are also the men at church who give me hugs. It's like having a lot of big brothers who make me feel loved and safe.

I keep wondering: How did I get so lucky to have men like these in my life? Then I think they, all but one, were friends of my husband. I think they are doing it for him.

Jul 12, 2012

Sewing by Hand

Chapter 25

My grandmother sat in her rocking chair with a kidney-shaped sewing board covering her lap and made shirts for my grandfather by hand. In her diary of 1892 she wrote, "Commenced Frank's shirt." A few days later there would be a notation, "Finished Frank's shirt."

I read these notations years ago but didn't give them a lot of thought at the time. Also, one of my older friends mentioned she had a friend who made all her clothes by hand. She didn't own a sewing machine. It wasn't until I was tired of crocheting and trying to knit that I thought about sewing by hand. Just sitting and watching television seemed such a waste of time, but I didn't want to give up my favorite programs. I couldn't just sit and enjoy myself. There was this need in me to keep my hands busy, so I went through boxes of material I had and started making baby quilts for a group in Auburn. I met these ladies at the YMCA where I took my husband for swimming. So, I not only had something to do, I could easily pass on what I made. It started a new phase in my life. I began to make blouses, nightgowns, and dresses for myself as well.

When my husband had to go to the hospital for surgery, I needed a short coat, and since I had suitable material, I made one by hand. I cut out the pieces at home, put them in a bag, and took them to the hospital. When my husband was awake, we talked. When he slept, I worked. I still have that coat. It makes me realize what the possibilities are and that "what goes around comes around."

Jul 19, 2012

It's All About the Weather

Chapter 26

Talk about irony. Here I am trying to read about the drought from a soaking wet newspaper. Even though my guy puts the paper in a plastic bag and ties it, the water still gets through. Oh, if we could but share some of this rain with those other parts of the country that need it.

It's been years since I have seen it rain so hard, with thunder and lightning too. I was going out to check on my sheep but heard a clap of thunder and decided to check them from a window. Those smart sheep were in the shed where they should be. They would be there, even without the thunder, because they don't like the rain.

To younger people, it will appear that this is unusual weather for this part of the country; but to me, it brings back memories of when I was a child and experienced the same type of thing.

We heard and saw several thunderstorms around Auburn and lots of rain. I was in grade school at the time, which would have been in the thirties. My sisters and I were scared of the thunder and lightning. So, one day my father took us out on the back porch to watch a thunderstorm off in the distance. He wanted us to be aware of the beauty of it and not be afraid of one of the world's spectaculars. Our fear eventually turned into a healthy respect.

It seems to me that there are cycles to our weather patterns. If so, those people who say there is nothing new under the sun are probably right.

Jul 26, 2012

Why Mothers Get Gray

Chapter 27

We were sitting around the kitchen table, three of my teenagers and a friend's boy, while this boy's dog, Blacky, waited for him by our gate near our newspaper box.

We were busy in conversation when a car drove up, and a boy hopped out to deliver our paper. Now, Blacky didn't particularly like paperboys, so he began to bark loudly.

Noticing from the window that the dog was barking at the paperboy, I suggested that the kids call off the dog. None of the teenagers made a move to do anything, and shortly the dog quit barking, whereupon my oldest daughter hollered out, "Spit him out Blacky!"

Note: Blacky was quite a dog. In fact, he was the only dog I ever took to the mall. On the day I was to take my son and his friend Bill, the dog's owner, to the mall, the dog wasn't in sight. I thought, oh good, I don't want a dog in my car. We started out, but after a block or so I noticed a black dog running down the street behind us. Now, Milton has a few hills, and as I watched in my rearview mirror, I saw this black dog top the rise on two of them, and he was still coming. It had to be Blacky. I told the boys if that dog comes over the next hill, I'm going back and pick him up. He came over that next hill, and so Blacky got to go to the mall, and the boys couldn't stop laughing.

Aug 02, 2012

Ask and It Shall Be Given You

Chapter 28

Having read this in the Bible many times, I still had doubts. What happened last week has given me a whole new perspective on it. Last Wednesday, I got an e-mail from the president of our group, the Milton Police Foundation, asking us to find more people to spell off the Police Chief in the dunk tank for the Milton Days celebration. My first thought was, how does she think we can accomplish that? Who in heaven's name would want to be dunked in a tank of water if they didn't have to? The Chief has a definite interest in doing it. He wants us to earn enough money for those flash cams we've been working for.

Then I went to my check-up appointment with Dr. McDonald. Always looking for something to make people laugh, I thought I'd ask him to be in the dunk tank. What a surprise! Instead of some kind of crazy excuse that we would laugh at for a while, he said, "I've done it before." And then he said, "If I'm not scheduled for that Saturday, or if I'm not on call, I'll do it." Big surprise! More like shock. My doctor that I've known for twenty plus years will actually do this just because he was asked. It's inconceivable.

Before I got over that, but emboldened by it, I asked the guy that does my yard work if he would do it, and he said yes. He'd have to rearrange his schedule for that weekend, but he'd do it. He'd also ask some of his buddies in the Lion's Club, and they would probably take a turn at it too. There are a lot of ifs there, but if they work out, we have it covered.

In conclusion, no matter what you think you know, just ask the question and see what you get.

Aug 09, 2012

Sister Lauretta Stops Traffic

Chapter 29

In these days of heavy traffic, I'm sure you will relate to Sister Lauretta's dilemma when her car died in the only left-turn lane in the middle of Federal Way during the Christmas rush. All of us who wanted to make a left turn to get to the freeway entrance were stuck behind her. With an island to the left of us and two full lanes to the right of us, we were in the neck of the bottle, and it was effectively plugged.

Poor Sister Lauretta was busily trying to get going again, which was duly noted by the smoke that was coming out of her car's exhaust. At first people honked their horns, but that did not help except to make Sister Lauretta try harder, thus sending out more smoke. So, they settled down, realizing that if progress could be made, it would have been done already.

The light changed twice. We who were behind her were looking to our right with the hope that some good Samaritan would let us in so we could go around her, but they were looking straight ahead. There was no eye contact. They evidently were afraid to look at us, because then they would have to do something about our plight.

Realizing that I wouldn't be clobbered if I got out of the car, I told my passenger I was going up there to see if I could help. When I got to the stuck lady's window and asked if there was anyone I could call to help her, she said "Yes. You could call Triple A." Then she began to rummage in her purse for what I thought would be her AAA card, but she came up with fifteen cents for the phone call. Then she found the card. I told her she didn't have to pay for the call, I'd take care of that. The main thing was to get her out of there. She, however, insisted.

She must have been praying awfully hard, for the minute I got back to my car, the cars in the next lane let me out, and I was able to get through the next light. I made my way to Safeway, where there was a pay phone. Calling AAA, I got some guy who asked several questions, and finally when he asked when does her policy expire, my Irish temper flared. "SHE'S GOT HALF OF FEDERAL WAY BACKED UP AT THE LIGHT! SEND THE TOW TRUCK! If you can't trust Sister Lauretta of the Sisters of the Holy Cross, who can you trust? Send the tow truck," and I banged the receiver down, got back in my car and went home to nurse a headache.

Aug 16, 2012

Saved by the Heat

Chapter 30

I needed some clean-up work done because of the destruction from last winter's ice storm. My neighbors hired a guy to trim and haul away branches and debris. Since my lawn guy doesn't do that kind of thing, I decided to get an estimate for cutting up the 6-8" branches that came down from the cherry tree and landed on my garden space. It was just that and some dead branches on the prune tree that needed to be sawed off and carried away -- just these two jobs.

The man came, and I showed him the cherry limbs. He said that he would have to have part of his crew come down and clean up the blackberries that were growing nearby before he could cut up the cherry limbs. Okay, that sort of made sense to me, although I thought one man could do it all. With a few good whacks, the vines would be out of the way. He put out his hand and I shook it. He said my fruit trees needed to be topped and trimmed. I didn't say anything and he put out his hand and we shook again. He looked at the fir trees and said they had two "widow makers" up there. I couldn't see them. If he had said there were branches that needed to come down on the roadside of the trees, I would have agreed with him. I knew there were branches there that looked suspect. He kept finding more things, shaking my hand about five times total. I thought he was too weird and decided not to hire him to do anything; but I was nice and said I'd let him know.

On Thursday, he called while I was gone and left a message telling me that it would be too hot on Friday to work with the gear they had to wear and they'd come next Friday to do the work. He didn't need to wear any gear to do what I wanted done, just a chain saw and a pickup truck, and I hadn't said yes even to that, I thought. I called my lawyer friend and asked about it and found out the truth. Had I been gone and the man ordered his men to do the work he said needed to be done, I would have been liable for the cost. It would have been his word against mine, and the fact that we shook hands would have been taken into consideration. My friend said that next time I ask for an estimate I should be forceful about just what work I want done and what I would pay for. I called this pushy guy, and after four tries he answered, and I told him not to come, that I did not have any money. I really stressed that. (After all money is the bottom line.) He said, "Have a nice weekend."

Aug 23, 2012

Miss Maginnis and Teaching

Chapter 31

School is starting, and that brings back fond memories of Miss Maginnis, my 7th grade English teacher and librarian. We hurried to get our work done so she could read to us. She had a real talent for that. The books she chose to read to us were always exciting, and she never failed to leave us in suspense when the bell rang and we had to go. We could hardly wait for the next time to find out what happened in the story.

Now, Miss Maginnis was Irish. She was a small woman who wore quite high heels and stood straight to get as much height as she could. She didn't need it. She had our respect regardless.

Her English assignments were a little different too. The one that stays in my mind was the one where we were supposed to stand up in front of the class and give a sales pitch. I wondered what to talk about and then hit on an idea, but I would have to ask her about it first. In art class, we had a lesson on soap carving. We had to buy a bar of soap and bring it to class. Dumb me; I bought a bar of Fels Naphtha. It was a caramel color but definitely smelled like laundry soap. In class, I tried really hard to make something nice out of that bar, but it didn't cut very easily, and I ended up with only pieces. Some were big and some small.

Taking it home to try again, I had to realize that I was not a carver, but I noticed that these small pieces looked like candy. So, I put them in a dish in the refrigerator and waited for my bachelor uncle to come, who always checked out the fridge first thing. He saw them and took one. It fooled him, until he bit into it. So, I decided to ask Miss Maginnis if I could use them for my sales pitch. She not only said yes, she added, "I'll take one, so everyone will think it's all right." The plan was set.

I trimmed the pieces into neat squares and wrapped them in cellophane. On the scheduled day, everything went as planned. After my talk, and it was known I had samples, everyone wanted one. Miss Maginnis got hers first, and hands were raised all over the room. After passing them out, there was a lot of coughing and spitting and a steady line out to the water fountain in the hallway. Although Mary Jane Ebling never spoke to me again, apparently no parents complained, or if they did, I didn't hear about it. I was not reprimanded for this, and Miss Maginnis, as far as I know, never lost her job over it. I couldn't help but wonder about this terrible thing we did, but now I understand. It was the best lesson in deceptive advertising that she could possibly give.

Aug 30, 2012

Thoughts of the Day

Chapter 32

In looking through old files, I came across a folder titled Thoughts of the Day, with clippings from the high school bulletins that were issued to all those who worked at Fife High School. It was probably put out by Mr. Belknap, the high school principal. These were printed on a Ditto machine and, therefore, were in a purple/blue ink. That does not change the humor in them. They are as good now as they were then; all capable of evoking a laugh, or at least a shake of the head in assent.

Examples:

Thinking is the hardest work there is, which is probably why so few engage in it.

Ideas die quickly in some heads, because they can't stand solitary confinement.

Success tip: Start at the bottom and wake up.

You don't have to stay awake nights to succeed. Just stay awake days.

The modern world thinks too much of its rights and too little of its responsibilities.

Too many of us conduct our lives on the cafeteria plan – self-service only

Ideas are funny little things; they won't work unless you do.

Some minds are like concrete – all mixed up and permanently set.

Education will broaden a narrow mind, but there's no known cure for a big head.

One thing about these "thoughts of the day," whoever wrote them knew a lot about teenagers, and Mr. Belknap would definitely fill that bill. He could take it as well as dish it out, too. The kids were very inventive. An example of what they did was cutting two watermelons in half the long way and putting a half under each of the tires on his Volkswagen, so when he started up to go home, all he could do was spin his wheels.

Final thought from the file: *The door of knowledge is labeled "Push."*

Sep 06, 2012

The Goodness in People

Chapter 33

Inez Robb, columnist, wrote that nine out of ten visitors carry away the conviction that New Yorkers are not always neighborly or friendly. She continues, a London columnist wrote to his paper that a New Yorker could drop dead on the sidewalk, and even his next of kin would simply step over the body and go about his business.

She refutes that by telling about a little five-year-old girl named Liza who lived in an apartment house where the water risers connecting the bathrooms carried sound perfectly. Liza's doctor prescribed vitamins for her but she didn't want to take them. Her poor mother tried, in the bathroom, for ten minutes pleading and threatening; but Liza protested loudly that she was not going to take them. The nice gentleman in the apartment above heard the goings on from his bathroom and proceeded in a strong and vibrant voice to say, "THIS IS GOD! TAKE YOUR VITAMIN PILL, LIZA," and she did.

Liza's mother wrote the old gentleman a note thanking him for what he did. His reply, "I am always happy to be of service in emergencies." (From the book Don't Just Stand There.)

How many times do we get the wrong impression about people and carry away a bad thought of them? I certainly did when some new people moved in across the street from me. I noticed that the young man had tattoos up and down both arms. Immediately, I thought he's trouble with a capital T. But was I wrong! Garbage day came, and after the last pick-up I went out to bring in my recycle bin and garbage can, and here was this young man picking them both up and carrying them down my driveway asking, "Where do you want them?" Not only that, he had a nice friendly grin. Now, for the last month, I have not had to bring in those containers. I don't see him do it. However, when I go out to get them, they are already in place. How about that!

We all know there are a lot of bad people in this world, but jumping to conclusions because of the way some dress or the way they appear to be can send us in the wrong direction. We need to look for that goodness in people that is surely there in the majority of us.

Sep 13, 2012

Cash on
the Barrel Head

Chapter 34

Today I cancelled a dentist appointment. My dentist requires that you have your teeth cleaned. As the dental hygienist cleans, she looks for problems and shows the dentist what she finds and he checks and confirms. After that you make another appointment for the work to be done. Since I don't have dental insurance and haven't required any to date, I pay as the work is done. Paying for the cleaning would be the first step.

The problem comes when you have other things in the works. I planned on taking my ready cash to pay for a new heating stove. The only problem is that I haven't been able to find one (or, rather, the heating guy that's looking hasn't found one) that will work in my old house. However, this nice man said he will remake my old stove, and it will work like it did before it wore out. (After all, it is over 60 years old.) The only thing this nice man and his crew tells me is they will take the old stove to their shop and have it back in two days, but they can't say what the charge will be. So, I'm in a holding pattern.

The dentist's receptionist, who called to remind me of my appointment, says I can make payments and doesn't understand that when you are on a fixed income, paying cash is better. You spend only when you've got the money, and if you pay the whole amount at the time, there are no fees or interest charges. There is no problem with waiting to have your teeth cleaned, either. So, I put it off until I find out what the stove will cost me.

When I ask those who will fix the stove what it will cost, the answer is, "Oh, it won't be very much." Now what is their idea of not very much? There could be quite a diversity between what they think is not very much and what I think is. My problem, as my lawyer friend tells me, is that I'm not forceful enough. When getting an estimate, I must be more insistent. But how do you tell the owner, a big 6'4" guy who seems like he is doing me a favor, that he can't get by with "it won't be very much" and demand a figure? He smiles a great smile, so I believe him and say nothing. We'll see how that works out.

Note: It worked out fine. I heard today what it's going to cost, and I'm happy. We are on the same wavelength. The stove will be back tomorrow, and I'm saving money. What could be better?

Sep 20, 2012

You May Be Eligible to Vote

Chapter 35

Today eleven hundred of us got cards from the Secretary of State's office encouraging us to find out if we were eligible to vote, and if we were, to register before the deadline for the next election.

What's this? When did things get changed? Wasn't I paying attention? If I'm not registered, how come we got those certificates, my husband and I, from Pat McCarthy for being faithful voters all those years? I got out my wallet and, yes, I had a voter identification card, and it said I registered August 8, 1952. That's right. I remember. My husband and I bought a house, moved in, had our first baby, and settled down to be good citizens, and then we went off to Milton City Hall and registered to vote.

Knowing that I was registered, I called the Secretary of State's office. What I found out didn't make me feel better. The person that answered said she had my name on her list but her copy was so fuzzy that it was hard to read. In fact, she thought my middle name was Jean, which it isn't. The card came addressed to LaVerna Conrad, no middle name or initial. Now where did they get that? She didn't know. This conversation was getting nowhere, except that we agreed I shouldn't have gotten the card because I was on the registered list. So I said goodbye and called the number on my card for the Pierce County office. He had everything right. Plus, he could read his copy and assured me I was registered and I would get my ballot on time. Not only that, he will make sure my middle initial is included.

Now that I'm sure I'll be getting a ballot, the question arises: whom will I vote for? That's a huge question this time around. Then comes the thought: will it make a difference? My 93-year-old neighbor, a naturalized citizen from Switzerland, is sure it will. She's angry with people who say they aren't going to vote. She worked hard for that privilege, taking the bus into Tacoma week after week to go to school to learn about our government. She knows more about it than most of us who were born here. So, if you're eligible, Mrs. Schorno says VOTE!

Sep 27, 2012

The Right
Frame of Mind

Chapter 36

When you have a son who is a policeman, you get a gun permit. I've had one now for several years. This was the year that it had to be renewed, so I went to our neighborhood police station to fill out the necessary forms so they could check up on me and make sure I deserved one.

Because it had been so long (five years) since I had done this before, I was not thinking on the same level as the people who make up these forms. For example, when they asked if I was known by any other names, I promptly said no, thinking only of nicknames. Wrong! She said, "You had a maiden name, didn't you?" Of course, I did but that was a long, long time ago. Surely, they can phrase that question differently.

Then there was the matter of scars. The questions went color of eyes, color of hair, height, weight, and then the question, "Do you have any scars?" Right away I naturally think they mean scars that show. After thinking it over, I told her I do have a mole under my right eye. Does that count? "No", she says. "Haven't you had some surgeries that left scars?" Okay, now they are definitely thinking in different terms than I am. This information can only be used to identify dead bodies. What other use can there be for this information? What do they think? If you own a gun you might accidentally shoot yourself? Or is it that when you own a gun they get the right to find out everything about you and keep it on file? No doubt they just want to be able to identify that the right person is the one using the permit.

The biggest question of all came when I received the permit. It was hand delivered on a Sunday afternoon by a stranger. She said it had come with her mail. It was in an unstamped envelope with the city's return address, and my name on it, in big bold letters. I'm sure wondering just what was the frame of mind of that person who mailed it?

Oct 04, 2012

Good Samaritans
Made My Day

Chapter 37

Sunday was like a usual day. Although I did miss church because I didn't hurry fast enough, the animals got fed and things got done. So, then I went to pick up a prescription at Safeway and after that to get some sheep feed from Del's Feed Store.

Going along the hillside to Del's, I found the road in the slide area to be worse than I had ever seen it. The concrete was quite broken up and very rough. I was glad I wasn't driving the Suburban. But that's all I thought about as I went on to the store.

I parked in the handicapped spot by the front door and went to make my purchase. We were almost through when she said, "You have a flat tire, and this man has offered to change it for you." I looked out the open door. Sure enough, my left rear tire was flat and there was a man standing close, in motorcycle gear, with helmet in hand, waiting to take care of it. She then said I could go over to the warehouse and tell the man there and he would bring the sack of alfalfa pellets to my car. Not one, but two Good Samaritans. I didn't have to go over there. He came to me and it was done.

It has been so long since I had a flat tire, I knew there was a jack that came with the car, but I hadn't even looked at it. I told him I had AAA, but not only was he willing to change the tire, another man came up with a canister of something that would seal the tire. So, then there were three Good Samaritans. My motorcycle guy opted for changing the tire because I could go further on it. He and his wife thought that was the best, because I would have to go somewhere to get the tire fixed after I got home. They also suggested that I go to the nearest gas station and get some air in the spare, because it seemed a little low, so that's what I did.

When I got to the station, I thought, gosh, I don't know how to do this. So, I went into the store and asked the lady behind the counter if there was someone there who could do it for me. She thought only a second, then came out from behind the counter, went out, and did it for me. But she showed me, in a very nice way, how it's done, so I can do it myself next time. So, then there were four Good Samaritans and one very grateful recipient.

Oct 11, 2012

The Closest I Came to a President

Chapter 38

Back in the thirties when I was attending Washington Grade School in Auburn, Washington, we were told the President was coming by. At the appropriate time, we were taken out to the front of the school so we could wave to him. There was this air of anticipation, and we could hardly wait until he'd get there. When his touring car, with the top down, came into view, we were told to wave, which we did, and he waved back. If I remember correctly, there were just two men with President Hoover and definitely no other cars. What a difference from then until now. He was probably in this region to campaign. We never knew, but that is my assumption now.

How far and wide this campaigning has gotten from those days. Now we can stand at the roadside where the President is traveling and wave, but we wonder which car in the motorcade he is in.

One also wonders about the money being spent during this campaigning time. After it's all over, what will happen? How many more people will be out of work because this money that went to hotels, restaurants, airlines, TV stations, and all the other supportive services is no longer coming in?

I'm not listening to debates or TV ads. They are not going to change my idea of who to vote for after checking their past performances. That seems more important than listening to any of the posturing they are doing now. However, praying for divine guidance in making the right decisions about who should govern us in the future seems the best way to go. I would suggest that everyone do the same.

Oct 18, 2012

Our Ghost Story

Chapter 39

The house I live in was built in 1909. Rooms were added to it in 1929. These are the things we can prove by clues left behind. There were also people named Amidon who lived here at one time, and that's what this story is about.

One day, I was reading the obituaries and saw that a man named Amidon, 76 years old, had passed away. It was maybe three days later that my husband and I were sitting in our living room watching television when we heard sounds coming from the front porch. It sounded like footsteps on the porch, but no one ever came to the front porch. Everyone comes to the back door, because that's where our driveway is.

It was as though someone was stomping up to the door. The screen door flew open, and then the front door flew wide open. We thought one of our kids had come to visit, but when I looked, no one was there. We were shocked. That door sticks; but here it was wide open, and no one had come in. Since I was closest to the door, I got up and closed and locked both the screen door and the front door. I don't know why I said it, but I turned to my husband and told him, "Mr. Amidon has come home."

Oct 25, 2012

Important Words

Chapter 40

My friend and I go to thrift stores every so often for something to do. Occasionally we find something we really want. Other times we get something that we aren't even sure what it's for, but if it looks interesting, we buy it.

On one occasion, I bought a plaque because it had colors that would go in our upstairs bathroom. I didn't even read what was on it. When I got home I cleaned it up and hung it in the bathroom.

At first, I didn't pay any attention to what it said. I was just satisfied that the colors matched others in the room, and it looked good hanging there. I guess I really didn't read it because it was in old English script and it took time to figure out what it said.

One day I took time to really look at it and read it. It said:

Do What You Can
Where You Are
With What You Have

I have read it every day since. Also, I found out that this is a quote of President Theodore Roosevelt. After my husband died and I was sitting here alone, I thought of those words and took stock. That ended up in the realization that I was living on a mini-farm. Which led to the thought of what I can do here. Since then I've had our old apple trees sprayed for worms and have been giving away apples. This year the crop is the biggest ever.

I have put four boxes of apples (windfalls) out by the road, and someone has picked them up in minutes. People have come from the church to pick the apples for themselves and others. A mother came yesterday with two of her six children to pick up the windfalls and help me pick up the bad apples for the sheep. It didn't matter that it was raining. They wanted to do anything they could to help me. They didn't realize that just coming to get something they could use helped me the most.

Nov 01, 2012

Strangers

Chapter 41

My father used to say strangers are just friends you haven't met yet. This was an important thing to say to us. Almost all people fit that category. There are a few, of course, that might do you harm, and you have to follow your instincts about that. Otherwise, give the strangers a chance.

I was in the Post Office to pick up my mail, and as I was leaving a little boy began to talk to me while his mother was at the counter mailing a package. Being a grandmother (actually "great" goes before that), I took time to listen to him. Understanding him was something else. However, "yes hm hm" or something similar suffices. Giving the child my full attention was my goal for a few seconds. The child was bubbling that he had something to share and someone listened to him. I was in my car when they came out, and that little boy was not smiling. He had been chastised. He had been talking to a stranger. How sad. We had had a moment that we both enjoyed, and it is my guess that it was spoiled because his mother is teaching him not to talk to strangers.

Years ago, my neighbor and I took our kids to a TV station in Seattle so they could be on Miss Elaine's program. Afterwards, since it was such a nice day, we went across the street to the park so the kids could play for a little bit. There were several old men sitting on benches and the kids are skipping and happy, so these fellows said hello to them as they went by and they said hello back and waved to them as they skipped along. When we got to where we were going, my friend told the kids not to talk to these old men. I saw no harm in it. I saw those old faces light up. Those kids made their day. How could that be bad? We were right there. Why not let them bring some joy into others' lives? People have to think of circumstances. There is that line between protection and being a good human being. If we expect to make this old world a better place to live in, we'd better figure out the difference.

Nov 08, 2012

Moving On

Chapter 42

Let's all breathe a sigh of relief. No more listening to political ads. Was it just me, or did it seem to go on forever? It must have been quite a shot in the economy to those places where the candidates visited a lot. Probably the total amount spent for all the campaigns would be in the billions. I wonder how close that amount would come to canceling out our national debt?

Well, it's over, and now we can look forward to the holidays. I especially like Thanksgiving because of the good times we have together. Family and friends are the best reasons for being thankful. Of course, there are many reasons to be thankful in this country. My new Ukrainian friend, Olga, who's been coming for apples, would be the first to agree.

We are fortunate and have so much to be thankful for. It is good that there is a day set aside just for expressing those thoughts for the people that mean so much to us, and for the gifts of love we receive from each other. Even though in many places Christmas is already on the scene, we will always celebrate this day and thank the Lord for our many blessings.

May you and yours have a wonderful Thanksgiving too!

Nov 15, 2012

Some Things Change - Others Not So Much

Chapter 43

No doubt different times, different circumstances change the way we look at things. Our family was recently given two high school annuals from Snoqualmie High School. One was for the class of 1926 and the other for 1927. There was a page of jokes in the one for 1926. Some of these jokes are timeless, and others – well, I guess you had to be there.

Some examples:

"Pardon me are you one of the teachers?"

"Gosh no! I got this tie for Christmas."

John Young—"Why did you stop singing in the choir?"

Landon—"Because one day I didn't sing and someone asked if the organ had been fixed."

She—"Can you drive with one hand?"

He—"You bet I can."

She—"Then have an apple."

As John Verhaus says in his book, The Comic Tool Box, comedy is truth and pain. If that's true, we should be laughing all the time, since there is an abundance of these components in life.

One of the latest jokes I've received is a picture of an old man with a rifle across his knees. The caption: "Just shot my first turkey. Scared everyone in the frozen food section. It was awesome! Getting old is so much fun."

Whether the jokes are over 80 years old or just made up this month, they make us laugh, and as it has been said, laughter is the best medicine.

Nov 29, 2012

Sears Just Couldn't Get It Right

Chapter 44

A few months after my husband and I married, we had a decision to make. His job was going away. The plywood plant he was working for was going co-op. In order to keep working there, he had to buy stock in the company. There was enough money to do that, but we had planned to use it for a down payment on a house. So, this was a big dilemma. After much discussion, we decided to buy the house, and he would look for another job. He applied and got a job with the Purex Corp. at $1.35 an hour.

This was a big cut in pay, but now we had our home. A farm house with fruit trees, berries, a place for a garden, and a mortgage that needed to be paid. It was hard times for us. Our families had us to dinner often, and I canned everything I could, so we were never hungry.

My mother helped in another way. Being so busy with a growing family, I didn't realize what she was up to. She would buy something from the Sears Catalog that didn't fit her or that she said she didn't like and then ask me if I could use it. It was just too much trouble to send it back, she said. I remember a nice white blouse as one thing she gave me. They had sent her the wrong size. When I was pregnant, I gained weight. After the baby was born, clothes I had didn't fit, so the blouse was needed. There was material she gave me and other things. The last thing she gave me was a cardboard wardrobe. Sears had done it again. She had ordered one with a shelf for hats and this one didn't have a shelf. It was something to give away. By then we needed a bedroom for our oldest daughter, who was five years older than her sisters and needed her own space. While my husband was working steadily, he still didn't make a lot of money at Purex, so he did a lot of moonlighting, taking any job he could. That didn't give him a lot of time to do things at home, but he bought some shelving from a store that was going out of business to use as a bookcase. With that we divided the living room for her bedroom. With the bookcase for one wall and Mother's wardrobe for the other, we had a bedroom for Anna Marie. It was that wardrobe that made the light go on, and I finally realized how much my mother had helped us for so many years and how she used Sears to do it. She never ordered another wardrobe. She didn't need one.

Dec 06, 2012

Nothing Says Christmas is Coming Like...

Chapter 45

Oh, if it were not so! However, the season is heralded by commercials advertising Chia Pets, The Clapper, The Ove Glove, and could we leave out the green bean casserole?

Where are the Christmas carols? Where is the Red Nosed Reindeer and the others that we have grown to love and expect? These are the things that really get us in the mood for this joyous occasion, the celebration of the birth of our Lord Jesus Christ.

Not only do we hear these commercial pleas to buy, but they are the same ones we heard last year and in previous years. I suppose it's all to save money while making more. These things have been made to be seasonal. So, they just run the same commercials again. Don't fall for them. This grandmother can do without any of these things. Pot holders I have. I'd forget to water a Chia pet (or herbs), and it's best to move, so that leaves out the Clapper. I'm so-so on the green bean casserole.

While I work on Christmas presents and address my cards, I'm turning off the TV and putting on my Christmas records. That will really put me in the true Christmas spirit. However, if a grandchild or great grandchild succumbs to this seasonal rush of commercialism, I'm sure I will love and cherish any of the aforementioned items. Not because of the gift, but because of the love of the giver. That, I will cherish forever.

Dec 13, 2012

A Christmas Challenge of Another Sort

Chapter 46

The last car was backing out of the driveway. It had been a wonderful Christmas Eve party as always. The ones in the last car had shut the driveway gate and now were backing out onto the road to go home. With a sigh, I tried to lock the door, but I couldn't. Something broke. My first thought was to run out and shout at that last car, but realized that it was too late. They would be out in the street and gone before I could get there.

My next thought was, it won't lock, and what will I do to be safe? I kept fiddling with the handle, and finally the bolt shot home. At least it was locked for the night. So far, so good, and I will work on this in the morning. Off to bed I went.

The next morning, I got ready to go outside and feed the sheep, and guess what. I couldn't unlock the door. The bolt had shot home last night, but there was no way to get it back out. I could go out the front door, but that presented problems, too, because I have trouble with my balance at times. I don't use the front entrance because there are thirteen steps to go down and no handrail. Then I remembered the time my husband and I had been stuck in my office in Federal Way. After thieves kicked in my hollow-core door, it was replaced by a solid core door. However, the old lock was not repaired, only replaced, and it broke. Fortunately, my husband was there when that happened, and he dismantled the lock to get us out. Remembering this, I got my screwdriver out and got busy. I was then able to get out by taking the lock apart. But what about a lock on Christmas Day? There was no way, and then I remembered something else. When my friend and I were shopping at a thrift store a long time ago, I bought a lock still in the package, still covered with plastic and all parts included. All I had to do was find it. Yep, it was there in my junk box in the jam cupboard.

I was busy working on this when my daughter Kay arrived. Together we did it. With a tool that looked like a tomahawk and a hammer, Kay chipped away and finally had enough wood out to make the part the bolt was to go into fit. We replaced the lock part after Kay's adjustment with the tomahawk and hammer to the wood on that side, and we had a lock that worked. Kay wanted her brother to know that she had met the lock challenge, and even though a woman, had taken care of the situation.

Jan 03, 2013

My Education Continues

Chapter 47

Sunday was football. Yes, I watched the game too, and wonder of wonders, they won. So now it's getting interesting. After so many years of losing at critical times, the Seahawks are winning, and I was right there at my TV set to urge them on.

It was great to see these guys all pumped up and playing at their best. However, it was a downer when Griffin's knee gave out and he had to leave the field. That brought back memories for me. That happened to my son in high school. He was playing football when he was sidelined because of a knee injury.

This was a learning experience for me like all others that had to do with the male gender. My husband could go down to the bench to see how he was. My son's girlfriend could go and see how he was. But I was told not to go down there at all. I don't know what the rationale was about that. Maybe if your mother showed up it would take away from your masculinity? It would forever cast you as a Mama's boy? Who knows? I never could figure that out and didn't ask. On Monday, I was too busy taking my son to the hospital to have the knee operated on. That part was up to me, and no one said anything about that. It was just expected.

Then I learned another lesson. Since I was working and had insurance, I figured that my Pierce County Medical would pay the bill for his surgery, and it did. However, as soon as they found out that my husband had insurance for the same thing, they wanted their money back from the hospital. So my husband's insurance paid the bulk of the bill, and my insurance paid the smaller amount. Even though I paid as much for my insurance as a man would, it was secondary to my husband's. I didn't waste any time thinking about this, because my son was working hard to get that knee in shape so he could turn out for wrestling. No wonder mothers get gray.

Jan 10, 2013

Life's Full of Surprises

Chapter 48

In going through a file of newspaper clippings, I came across one with the headline, "The FEDs Studying Recall of 9 Million Fords."

The article explained that The National Traffic Safety Administration began an investigation after the Independent Center for Auto Safety said 100 accidents were caused by the transmission in those cars (between 1973 and 1978), jumping from park to reverse by themselves, and twelve people had been killed.

Now this would have been hard for me to believe if I'd read it before it happened to me. Instead, I've saved this article because it did happen. At that time, the mail boxes for everyone on our street were just up a little hill from the highway. I came home that day, turned off the highway and parked on top of the little hill, shut off the motor, put the car in park, and got out to get the mail. We had quite a bit, and I stood going through it to be sure it was all ours. While I was standing there, I heard a crunch of gravel, but I didn't think anything about it because our road was always well traveled.

When I finished checking, I turned to cross the street to my car, and it wasn't there. Instead it was rolling down the hill toward the highway. I began chasing it. It went down, crossed the highway, and was going up the other side with me in hot pursuit. When it got as high as it could go, it stopped, and I caught up with it, opened the door, and got in. Just as if I'd planned it that way. Started it up, put it in gear and drove home.

If anyone saw that little episode, they must have thought it was hilariously funny; but I guess you know I wasn't laughing.

Jan 17, 2013

Technology Can Make Trouble

Chapter 49

Where does Google get the information that they use on their site? When I was told there was a LOT of information on me, including a picture of my house, I decided to check it out. Though I didn't see that picture, I saw so many listings and wrong information, including that I was the owner of Caldwell Banker Real Estate in Sumner. That's when I quit looking at the site.

Major Oliver Conrad, retired (no relation), started selling real estate in Lakewood, and he had Coldwell Banker Real Estate precede his name in the phone book. Unfortunately, my name came before that, so people thought we were in it together. That's when I began to get the mailings, phone calls, and messages left on the recorder. It took calling Major Conrad, retired, and having a little talk with him about how things work in the phone book and how upset I was with all the wrong attention I was getting. There was the rancher in Idaho that sent me a flyer wanting to sell his 1500-acre ranch at a reduced price. Then there was the man who left a message on my tape telling me he had a good list of people in my area that were ready to buy and he would only charge me $10.00 a name. After a while of my hanging up on people, writing to inform others I was not in the real estate business, it went away.

Now with this thing on Google, I imagine it will all come back and I will have to fight it all over again. But maybe I should rethink this and take up selling real estate. It could be more lucrative than writing. After all, John Steinbeck said that writing for a living made horse racing seem like a good solid business, and I guess he knew whereof he spoke.

Jan 24, 2013

When the Baby Died

Chapter 50

In this segment, I have to set the record straight. At a meeting of the Milton Police Foundation, I made a statement that I want to clarify. In asking if our Police Department had a chaplain, I stated that policemen call their mothers when there is no chaplain. From this, people might think my son called me whenever he was troubled about something he encountered on duty. I want to make it clear that he only called me once: the day the baby died.

The mother knew the baby was sick and made an appointment with the doctor for 1:00 p.m. She left her babysitter in charge and went to work. The sixteen-year-old babysitter, making her usual check, found the baby had turned blue and called 911.

My son was patrolling in the area, so he was first on the scene. He knew the baby was dead. There was no heartbeat and the blood had pooled. The baby sitter was frantic, and my son knew he needed to do something for her, so he began to give the baby mouth-to-mouth.

Within a short time, the baby's skin began to turn a little pink, and he thought maybe he was wrong. Maybe the child could be brought back. So, he had a little hope, too. However, when the medics came, there was still no heartbeat. At 1:00 a.m. the baby was pronounced dead at the scene. All my son had been able to do was give the girl a little hope. No doubt this was the worst thing that had ever happened in her life, and she needed a little time to get her mind around it; when everything is done that can be done with the outcome, the same acceptance maybe came a little easier. I don't know.

It's hard to remember what I said to him at the time. Probably it was the usual mother thing of consoling, but I'm sure I told him he was right in what he did. Now, having had more time to think about things, I believe producing hope, even for a few minutes, can make an awful lot of difference.

Jan 31, 2013

Low Fill and Questions

Chapter 51

When my husband started working for The Purex Corporation, he was put on the line. His job was to put open boxes over the filled bottles of bleach as they came down the belt. Later he progressed to working the line where, if a bottle wasn't filled to the top, it would be taken out. That way a customer would not get a bottle that didn't have the right amount in it. They called these bottles "low fills".

Now, in our day it seems like we are confronted with low fill all the time. Apparently, this is the way companies raise the price -- by not giving you as much in the same container. You are paying the same price but are getting less for your money.

Yesterday I finally made it to Winco, my favorite store for good prices. There were several things on my list and my bill came to $74.64. Not bad, since I had not gone last week and had forgotten breakfast food when I went the week before. The surprise came when I began to put things away, especially the breakfast food. Talk about low fill. It would take two Raisin Bran boxes to fill up my plastic container, when one would have done it before. There was a little left in my Tupperware container, so I couldn't just dump out the contents and weigh it to see if it was the same amount that they have on the box. Probably it was, but next time I will check. Now I wonder how do they decide low fill when they are putting less in the box to begin with?

It also makes me wonder if Weights and Measures are doing their job. Surely, they are, but how can they tell? The job must be monumental with all the products available on grocery shelves. Thinking about that, I decided to stop and check their web site. I found they are involved in a lot of things. Hopefully they are busy doing the right things and protecting us in the process.

Feb 07, 2013

With This Ring, I Thee Wed

Chapter 52

My husband and I exchanged rings when we married, and we always wore them until my husband took a job painting a house with our neighbor.

Dick and the neighbor took as many part-time jobs as they could to add to their family's income. That's why, on a Saturday, they were in South Tacoma painting an old two-story house for an insurance man. It had taken all day, and it was late when they came home.

On the way home, our neighbor Bernard said, "You know that stuff we cleaned our hands with was so slippery I almost lost my wedding ring." Dick looked at his hand and his ring was gone. Bernard said, "Let's go back and look for it now." But Dick said no. He took Bernard home, stopped to tell me what was going on, and went back to look for his ring.

He searched until it was too dark to see, and then came home. He obviously felt bad about the ring being gone, and I told him the kids and I would buy him another one. He said, "No, that ring means too much to me. Another one wouldn't be the same."

Next morning he was up early and left to go back to the house. The lawn hadn't been cut and was quite overgrown. So, he cut and sifted the grass around the faucet all morning and about noon found the ring.

Coming home all smiles, he held up his hand with the ring on it as he came in the yard. Dick was so happy that he had found this symbol of our love and commitment. I think I was the happiest though, because what better proof could a woman have of a man's caring and love for her and their life together than this.

Feb 14, 2013

Do You Have a Look Alike?

Chapter 53

It has been said that everyone has a double. My experience says that statement may be true. Back about 1948, a clerk at People's Store in Tacoma told me I looked just like a woman from Puyallup. She was certain that woman was my double. Okay, I thought, that's interesting, and I filed it away in my memory.

In the seventies, I was grocery shopping at Piggly Wiggly in Fife when a woman said hello and started a conversation about some event I knew nothing about. She realized I was not the person she thought I was and told me that I looked just like a friend of hers. She said this friend worked in the Lutheran Church in Puyallup. At that time, I was working as the secretary at the Fife Presbyterian Church -- what a coincidence. My first thought was I must go down there and meet my double. I did find the Lutheran Church, but the day I went, there was no place to park, so I gave up.

Last Sunday I went to a birthday party for a friend where over two hundred people were in attendance. I hadn't been there twenty minutes when a woman I'd never met or seen before came up to me and said, "You look just like a woman I know that lives in Milton, and she's going to be here today."

This was surprising, but having been told twice before that I had a double, I thought maybe at last I will find out who this person is. It was a very nice party, and as I was leaving, the woman came up to me again and said, "The woman I told you about is here. You must meet her." So, she takes me over to the woman who is about my height. Same hair color (though I wear a wig and she doesn't). Same color of eyes, but she is much slimmer, and to me we are not alike at all. She says she has never lived in Puyallup but lived in Milton for fifty years, where I have lived for sixty years. You'd think in all that time, if there was a resemblance, it would have been mentioned before. However, I ask her if she ever worked in the Lutheran Church in Puyallup. She said no and turned her back to talk to someone else, and I went home to ponder if I would ever meet my double -- or in fact, if there really is one.

Feb 21, 2013

The "Dam People"

Chapter 54

Back in the forties, Mud Mountain Dam was built for flood control. Since Enumclaw was the closest town, families moved in who had people working on the project. They were soon called "those Dam People." Probably this was to distinguish the temporary residents from the permanent ones, but it wasn't always used as a good term.

There was no difference, however. These people rented homes, sent their kids to the local schools, and lived like the rest of us. One of their boys was voted President of the Student Body one year. No doubt there were other kids that excelled in sports and other activities at school. The mothers got jobs, joined clubs, and saw that their families went to church.

One of these women was Betty Millan. I met her when I joined the Business and Professional Woman's Club. At that time, I was a secretary to the grade school Principal in Enumclaw. We saw each other at meetings but didn't really get to know each other until many years later when we met again at the Fife Presbyterian Church. We ended up as a team who counted money on Sunday, kept records, and took the money to the bank. We both loved this job. After we got the work done, we talked and laughed a lot about things that happened in Enumclaw and caught up on what had happened to us since we left there.

We had no idea volunteering for this job at church would bring us such benefits: talking together in a quiet atmosphere and being able to bring out things that were hurtful years ago but now found to be plain laughable. It's funny how time can make things mellow out. Another lesson learned.

Feb 28, 2013

Praying for Rain

Chapter 55

Moss has been invading my place. It is taking over the lawn. The sidewalks are covered with it. It has left a blanket of its finest on the concrete edge of the patio. There is even a little forest in the fork of an apple tree, where ferns grow out of it, in a little ecosystem. There are splotches of it on the roof. It's probably other places, too, that I haven't found yet.

A few years ago, I bought a sack of moss killer with lawn fertilizer in it and spread that in one section to experiment. Soon the moss in that area was dead and black. This time it was too late for that, so I called Pete's Spray Service. I was fixing my hair the next morning when there was a knock on the door. Not dressed yet, I put on my bathrobe and went to the door. It was Pete's Spray Service just come to measure the lawn. These guys are prompt. On cold mornings, I'm not. We established what they were there for, and I went back upstairs to get dressed. When they were done, they wisely called me on the phone and gave me the estimate, and I told them to go ahead. They said they needed rain to do it and told me I should pray for that.

Being one of those people who believe in praying for all things, I agreed. What I was praying for was RAIN. Tuesday there wasn't any. Wednesday there had been a sprinkle during the night, but nothing when I went out to feed the sheep.

Sitting in my chair, eating my breakfast, and listening to the news, I caught a slight movement out my kitchen window. Since I knew the sheep would still be eating their hay, I went to check. Here were the spray people doing their job. I asked one, "Didn't you say you needed it to rain?" He held out his hand and said, "It is." To me that was hardly a sprinkle. I looked at the sidewalk. It was barely wet. Right then I decided next time someone tells me to pray for rain, I'll have to ask them to be more specific. Do they mean RAIN rain or a light drizzle? You live and learn.

Mar 07, 2013

Partners

Chapter 56

Policemen have to work closely together for their protection and the protection of others and therefore develop a close bond. This was the case with my son and the person he worked with. They are buddies for life.

While they were working, funny things happened to them as well as bad things. One time I heard they had to check out a warehouse. Mike, my son, had been there before, but Roger hadn't. Going through the office to get to the main part of the building, Mike turned to Roger saying, "Don't let the door shut or we'll be locked in." Too late. Roger had let go of the door, and it slammed shut. They had to call someone to get them out. They probably heard about that one for a long time.

Both are retired out of the police force now, but they still are there for each other. At my husband's funeral, when Mike got up to give the Eulogy for his father, Roger stood beside him, and as Mike's voice filled with emotion, I heard Roger say, "I've got your back."

Now it's Mike's turn. Roger's mother died last week, and the funeral is Wednesday in Yakima. Mike will be there to stand by Roger.

These guys faced guns, knives, and as a state patrolman said at Mike's retirement party, "They tried to kill him a dozen different ways." Still, burying their loved ones has to be the hardest thing they've ever had to do. But they'll get through this too, because they have each other's back.

Mar 14, 2013

Men and Weed Eaters

Chapter 57

What is it about men and power tools, especially weed eaters? When they get their goggles on and that tool in their hands, they mow down everything in sight. Apparently, for them there is no distinction between grass, weeds, and flowers. I thought it was just my husband who had a problem telling the difference, but I find others don't get it either. Or are they just overcome with the power of their tool and the ability it has to level all plant life?

I don't get around to weeding my flowerbeds like I should. However, each spring gives me another chance to catch up. Seeing that my little bunch of tulips were coming up out by the back gate, I was hopeful this year. Then mowing day came. Not paying attention to what my lawn maintenance guy was doing, I stayed in the house to catch up with my writing project for the critique group. There were noises as small particles hit the side of the house. But, fully engaged in plotting my novel, I ignored them.

After he left, I went out to enjoy a newly mowed lawn. Then I discovered what he had been up to. The bush next to the house that looks like a Forsythia, but blooms in the winter, had been trimmed, even though it still had blossoms on it. That was what was hitting the house. The weed eater even works with bushes. Then I noticed he had been weed eating out by the back fence where my tulips were coming up. I rushed over to check their fate. They had gone the way of the weeds in that bed. Everything was neat and level. Now the lawn and flowerbeds are all the same height. But my tulips and I were crushed. Well, maybe next year I'll have tulips.

I don't know why I thought he could differentiate between grass and tulip leaves. He couldn't see Rhubarb leaves last year, either, and my whole row of Rhubarb got "weed eaten" out of existence. Your first thought is why don't I fire him? He's a good guy and he works for the amount I can afford. Besides, would any other man be different? I don't think so. If you know of a woman in the business who works for cheap, let me know.

Note: All apologies to my son-in-law Kirk, who is an excellent gardener and probably doesn't even own a weed eater.

Mar 21, 2013

Adherence to a Faith

Chapter 58

In my scrapbook there is this quote: "Adherence to a faith makes a better person." I don't know who wrote it, but I think that person was on to something.

Many people feel there is a decline in our nation. There is definitely a decline in church attendance. Last Sunday I planned to go to church, but I slept in. So, then I had a problem. I could be late to my own church, or go to a church in my neighborhood and be on time. Since it was Palm Sunday, I decided to be on time. I was there in five minutes, expecting to find a packed church. That was not the case. There was just a sprinkling of people. I sat by the only person I knew, and we were the only two in that pew. Several other pews were empty. My own church, Sunrise Methodist, has seen a decline in membership and monetary support too. There is talk that if changes don't come about soon, drastic measures will have to be taken.

This is sad for a variety of reasons. In looking for the above quote, I also found this prayer in my scrapbook. I'd like to share it with you to put this into perspective.

MY PRAYER

I know three things must always be
To keep a nation strong and free.

One is a hearthstone bright and dear
With busy, happy loved ones near.
One is a ready heart and hand
To love and serve and keep the land.
One is a worn and beaten way
To where the people go to pray.
So long as these are kept alive
Nation and people will survive.
God, keep them always everywhere
The hearth, the flag, the place of prayer.

--Author Unknown

Mar 28, 2013

What to Call Yourself?

Chapter 59

Recently a woman's face lit up when she recognized me. I thought, she knows I'm Mrs. Conrad; but no. She said, "Oh, you're the sheep lady." Of course, I'm that too. We all are known for a variety of things. You get married and you're a wife or husband. Or you don't get married and you're committed to someone and become a significant other. You become a mother or father. Your children grow up and get married, or become committed to someone, and it starts all over again.

Suddenly, mother-in-law or father-in-law doesn't always fit. Or in the case of mother-in-law, it has a bad connotation, and you prefer not to be called one. So, what do you do? Well, at first you dance around it and try not to get into a situation where you have to use a name. Then you go the formal route, signing "Mrs. Conrad". That doesn't seem right either. So, you finally ask your daughter-in-law, "How should I sign the cards I send you?" We decided that first-name basis was best. That, too, seemed too casual, considering the difference in our age. Oh, what to do?

At long last I have come up with what I think is the best solution. I am now signing my cards, letters, and e-mails to my children's loved ones as (DRUM ROLL PLEASE) 'Your Other Mother". It kind of has a ring to it, don't you think?

Already I can hear comments that aren't exactly complementary to mothers. "You sound just like my mother." "You're turning into your mother." So, there is a bad connotation here, too. However, there is that better aspect of mothers. that loving, giving, caring person my mother always was and that I have tried to be. Hopefully, my other children (in-law) will see it that way as well.

Apr 04, 2013

The Space Needle - A Northwest Treasure

Chapter 60

From the time the Space Needle was built fifty years ago, I thought it would be nice to eat in the restaurant and be able to take advantage of the view from that height. It was the one place where it wouldn't matter where your table was. You would be able to see the complete view, because the restaurant revolves around a central core and has large windows on the outside.

Valet parking is provided at the base of the Space Needle, so there is a minimum of walking. The Cadillac of elevators takes you to the entrance of the restaurant in 41 seconds, and no funny feeling in the pit of your stomach when you get there. All of this I found out last Sunday when my dream of going to the Space Needle was realized. My children took me there for brunch. Since my grandson, Jacob, works there, we were able to meet the head chef, and also Jacob was able to come out and talk to us for a few minutes. We were not only able to talk to him, but got to see his uniform as well.

Besides the spectacular view, the food is great. The bacon is made there. In fact, Jacob takes it through all the processes, and that bacon is delicious. I expected a lot of salt like you find in the bacon you buy, but that was not the case. (My doctor will be happy to hear that.) The prime rib was also excellent. The best part was that the food was good the next day as well. The portions at restaurants seem to be much larger these days, definitely more than I can eat at one sitting. So, I get a "doggy bag" and reheat the food the next day. Sometimes it just isn't worth bringing home, because the food loses flavor when reheated, but not what I brought home Sunday. The mashed potatoes, veggies, and Prime Rib were just as delicious reheated as they were originally.

The people who waited on us were jovial and helpful. That always helps the digestion. It definitely leaves you in a good mood. All in all, this was a wonderful experience, and I publicly thank my family for providing this best of gifts.

Apr 11, 2013

Some Days are Diamonds, Some are Prune Pits

Chapter 61

Tuesday was all prune pits. Monday, I found out a window in the Carryall was broken. The person that brought it to my attention thought a BB had caused the tiny hole and shattered the glass. So after he left, I called the police. When the officer arrived, I went out to greet him and get his opinion on whether someone's been shooting at me or not.

He looks at it. He touches the hole while I wait expectantly. Then he gives his verdict. "I have seen many bullet holes and holes made by BB's, and this is neither. It's my thought a rock hit it."

Okay, then. The lawn mowing guy and his friend were here Friday. No mystery at all. The lawn mower did it. Now comes the problem of getting it fixed. I call a place that fixes wrecked cars. They do, but a guy named Matt comes and does the windows. So, I need to call Matt's company.

I call and get Linda. Her company would be happy to fix the window, but first they have to get the replacement glass. She will check and call me back in a few minutes. Of course,

I'm sure she has gotten my name and other essentials to check my credit.

A couple of hours pass by, so I call her and get the bad news. Glass for a vehicle that old is no longer made. She says I need to go to a wrecking yard and maybe I can find a panel there. So I call my mechanics, and they give me names of a few. I call one. Yes he has a panel that is for a 1986 Chevrolet Suburban and he can send it right away. Send it? Can't I come and get it? Then it comes out. He's in Oregon. He would send it to a shop in Spanaway for $50.00. I'm thinking no way! I'm not going to be driving around Spanaway hunting for a wrecking yard. That was the end of that conversation. (Anyway, I thought $50.00 was a bit pricey.)

The broken window is no longer important, because when I got up Tuesday morning, I found my front room stove had spewed a pile of soot out the back. Soot will take precedence over anything. My past experience taught me never to try and vacuum soot. It goes in one side of the vacuum and goes right out the other, spreading like a cloud. Therefore, I called the man who fixed the stove. He'll be here Saturday to assess the situation. And on the window problem, my lawn mower guy gave me a number of a wrecking yard in his neighborhood, who will call to let me know if he has a glass panel that will fit. So, prune pits aside, it's a waiting game all around. How to deal with this? Sit back, relax, take a nap, and ignore. At least I'll be rested when something finally gets done.

Apr 18, 2013

Having Second Thoughts

Chapter 62

At the end of the school year last June, someone blew up our neighbor's ornamental mailbox. A week later, a bomb went off in the night, and the mangled pipe from the bomb landed in my driveway, where my lawn guys found it the next day. In talking to our police chief, I found that a bomb had also gone off up above us on Meridian Avenue about twenty minutes before the one on our street was set off.

At the time, our neighbors were not so upset about their cute little mailbox being blown up. It needed fixing, and the husband was no longer able to do the work. Although the neighbors reported it to the police, they did not intend to pursue it and press charges if they found out who did it. They were just glad to get rid of the mailbox without having to do anything.

In my case there was no mention about who did it. The police officer just talked to Glen, who found the pipe, and then took it to the station to be turned over to Alcohol, Tobacco and Firearms people. I was told they preferred a bomb that hadn't exploded, and I hoped I would never find one.

Life went on and I forgot all about it. It didn't even occur to me when I heard about the Boston bombings. My neighbor, however, did think about it. She called me Friday. Now she and her husband realize that someone could have been badly hurt. Parts of that little mailbox and what blew it up were spread out. A piece was found in a window well on the side of their house, a good 30 feet away, and another piece was halfway up the hill by their neighbor's house. Other small pieces were scattered on their driveway and lawn. The policeman that took the report thought it was an M-80 (a big firecracker) that blew it up. Now my neighbor wonders if it was. Was it a prank? Or was someone practicing for something else? Because it was graduation time and kids get drunk and do dumb things, it's easy to think that was the cause. However, hearing about the bombing in Boston makes one think and wonder. It isn't likely that bombings a week apart were the result of a teenager's drinking party. So, now we all are questioning and wishing we knew who, what, and why of our little experience. We'll probably never find out. We do know one thing. These bombs were probably not intended to hurt anyone because of the time they were set off. Therefore, we will set them aside to include with other mysteries of life. Of course, if something like this ever happens again, we'll not ignore. We'll go for questions and insist on answers. The Boston bombings have been a lesson.

Apr 25, 2013

A Cure for
Tennis Elbow

Chapter 63

My right arm was hurting, so I went to see the doctor. His diagnosis: tennis elbow. I was to wait and the nurse would be in to put a brace on my arm. When she came, I was surprised. The brace was just a strip of heavy material with Velcro straps to hold it together. When I asked her what that was supposed to do, she said, "It's supposed to hold your bones together."

That's interesting, I thought. The doctor came back in and told me I'd have to wear the brace for a couple of weeks, and I'd have to come back for therapy on the arm.

That weekend, my husband and I went to Othello to visit our son and his family and also go to the Adams County Fair. Our daughter-in-law and the children were already at the Fair showing their animals, and our son was home doing some needed repairs. My husband decided to help with the welding and fixing, but there was a need for someone to rake a hayfield. Guess who got that job?

"Mother you can do it." I wasn't so sure. He got out the stepladder and helped me get into this monstrous beast of a tractor. Then he showed me how to run it. After it was running, I was to get it up to so many RPM's and then engage the gear, and the centrifugal rakes would start raking. I wasn't too sure yet about what to do, so he went over it again. Then in my female mind I figured it'll come to me while I'm doing it, so I took off.

At one end of the field was a little hill. My son had warned me to shut off the rakes, go up the hill, and turn around. Then come back down on the next row, get up to the right RPM's, and start the rakes again. I was actually getting the hang of this and was on the next to last row when something on one of the rakes broke, and before I had sense to shut it down, the broken rake had bored itself into the ground like a corkscrew.

Now my son had another thing to fix and weld; but first he had to dig it out of the ground. Almost every story has something good in it though. In this one it was shifting those gears that took care of my tennis elbow. When I got home, I didn't have to have therapy.

May 02, 2013

A Mother's Story

Chapter 64

Cheryl adopted a little baby girl some twenty years ago. Bringing her home when she was twelve days old, Cheryl loved and cared for her as any birth mother would. All the baby's needs were taken care of, and pictures were always taken to remember the important moments of this little girl's life.

When she was the right age, Cheryl took her for dance lessons. She also made her outfits for dance recitals. Piano lessons were also provided. As a mother, she was involved in school things as well, making sure her little girl took part in as many school activities as possible. In other words, she did everything for this child that other moms do. As a result, this little girl grew up to be a lovely young lady that Cheryl is so proud of.

However, Cheryl noticed that something was bothering her daughter. In talking with her about it, she found that the girl did not feel right about not knowing her roots. She wanted to know why her mother gave her up. Was she just abandoned? What had happened? They decided together they would find the birth mother and get answers to these questions if at all possible.

The daughter had gone online and found some information, and with what clues Cheryl had about this woman, they were able to locate and contact her. They were apprehensive about it, but it proved to be the right thing. The birth mother was overjoyed to hear from them. So, three weeks ago, Cheryl and her daughter flew to Louisiana to meet the woman who had given birth and had had to give her baby away.

Cheryl's daughter was not only able to meet her birth mother, but also to meet her grandparents, aunts and uncles, and lots of cousins. She knows now her mother didn't just abandon her. She was in a bad situation and wanted her to have a better life than she could give her. The father? Well he was married and never knew he'd fathered this child.

Cheryl gave the birthmother the book filled with all those pictures of her daughter's early years, so she could enjoy those important moments in her daughter's life. Now Cheryl is putting more pictures together for her so there won't be any gaps, and the birthmother will have the next best thing to being there.

May 09, 2013

Treasured People

Chapter 65

Odell Wallace is one of my treasured people for his "act of kindness" many years ago. He was the pharmacist at the Fife Rexall Store when this happened. There was something I needed that I couldn't get in Milton, and the clerk told me she was sure I could find it at the Fife store. That's why I was there.

At that time, I was the mother of four children five years old and younger. We had little money. My husband had had to change jobs earlier in our marriage, and his pay still wasn't up to where it had been. We were getting along, but we had nothing extra. I was wearing a clean cotton housedress and worn shoes, no make-up on, my straight hair pulled back in a ponytail fastened with a rubber band, and I carried my old worn purse.

The clerks were busy, of course, but they kept ignoring me, waiting on others who came into the store after I did. My self-esteem was quickly evaporating, and I stood there wondering what to do. I knew the tears were not far behind, and then suddenly here was the pharmacist at my side asking if he could help me find what I needed. He had come down from his perch in the back of the store and come clear to the front where I was, to help me. His smile and kind manner told me everything. In spite of how others looked at me and judged me, his actions said you are a good human being worthy of respect. He helped me find what I was looking for, and I thanked him. He responded with something like, "Glad to do it." Then said, "Have a good day," and went back to his station.

I no longer felt like crying, and now I could hold my head up. Odell Wallace had done a great deed that day and helped me beyond measure. Since I never told him he helped me so much, he probably didn't realize it. At the time, I didn't even know his name. I was to find that out years later when my husband and I moved our family to the Fife Presbyterian Church, where he and his family were members.

I'm writing this now because Odell passed away a week ago surrounded by his family. There will be a service on May 24h at the Little Church on the Prairie. Rest in peace, Odell. You've earned it.

May 16, 2013

Tips on Saving and Spending

Chapter 66

The first thing is, if it's not necessary, don't buy it. Everybody wants some of your money. Learn to say, "NO." Don't put off repairs. Keep things in good order. If you don't fix things, as you need to, they just get worse and cost more to repair. Then when you can't do without something and have to fix it (say a car to get to work), you not only pay for repairs but probably lose some pay because of no transportation.

My husband worked for a chemical company (Purex) but was paid warehouseman's wages, which were much less than chemical workers. Therefore, several times they went on strike. Whenever I knew a strike was forthcoming, I went on my strike-spending plan. In other words, saving money before I needed to, then spending it carefully and making the plan work when I had to.

There were six of us to feed, and that was my major problem, how to stretch strike pay (or lack thereof) to make sure everyone got the best possible diet at the lowest cost. Trying to spend only $10.00 a week on food, I first bought a pound of stew meat. Using our pressure cooker (a wedding present), I was able to cook some of it and called it steak.

The next day, I cooked some more and called it roast. The last day, I made stew with the remainder. Lettuce was usually inexpensive, so there was often a salad. You could get day-old bread, vegetables, and fruit that were past their prime, therefore cheaper in price. Then there was macaroni, spaghetti, and hot sauce that helped fill stomachs, so I could make my plan work.

This plan did not come out of my brain. My Home Economics teacher, Mrs. Agnes Horn, prepared us for just such a problem by giving us an assignment on feeding a family of six on 25 cents a day. Actually, she made it a contest, and I remember that Dorie Smith won that contest. The basic part of Dorie's plan was buying day-old bread, celery root, and over ripe fruit. I'm sure there were other things on her list also, but it's just too far back for me to remember everything.

However, the fact that it could be done was the motivating factor in my life. Mrs. Horn and Dorie had shown the way. All I had to do was check out prices and what was in season plus check what was in the rack of shopworn but still good packages of what we could use. I was usually surprised at how far my $10.00 would go.

If you're facing a possible layoff, start making a plan and start saving. If you only put all your coins in a jar every day, you'll be surprised at how it can add up. Besides, it will be good for your attitude, because you are doing something. Everyone knows that attitude is everything.

May 23, 2013

Repurposing

Chapter 67

Repurposing is the newest fad. The idea is to keep things out of the landfill. I'm all for it. However, it is nothing new to me. It seems I've been doing this all my life.

Back when my sisters and I were in school and all shared a bedroom, we decided to make a dressing table. We had seen them in magazines and in the movies, so we knew what they should look like. That's when we set about to make one.

It was summer time and we didn't have anything else to do, so we threw ourselves wholeheartedly into this project. We were lucky. We had a wonderful piece to work with. Our folks let us use our grandmother's lapboard. She had sat in her rocking chair with this board on her lap and did her sewing. In her diary she would write, "Commenced Frank's shirt." A few days later another entry would appear along with local items, "Finished Frank's shirt." She had no sewing machine. All the work was done by hand.

We took the lapboard and put it on top of two upended orange crates. Now orange crates were great for this, because they were divided in the middle by a board, so when you upended them, you had a shelf. The lapboard was kidney shaped, and to that we added flour sack material for a skirt. (The flour sack material came in patterns and was used for many things.)

So, there we had our dressing table. Now, every dressing table had to have a bench, so our next project was to find something to use for that. Our father came up with a butter box. It was perfect. These square butter boxes were solidly built. You could sit on any side of it, and it would hold up. We glued strips of flannel on the bottom edge of the box so it wouldn't scratch the floor, padded the top side, and covered it all with matching flour sack material, and it was ready for use.

Repurposing comes into play for artwork as well, and a lot of interesting things appear on the scene. When I repurpose, it's usually for a reason. Like the time our son and his wife asked us to go backpacking in the mountains with them. In the northwest, you never knew what to expect weather-wise, and in backpacking you don't carry anything extra. So, my hat had to work for sun or rain. The solution, a straw hat with a plastic liner. At that time, potted plants came in just such an item. I took one of these, turned it over, attached a cloth flower to the bottom (which was now the top), added a hatband, and I was all set to go. It was obvious that people wondered about that hat, but no one who saw it had guts enough to ask about it.

May 30, 2013

The Game of Gossip

Chapter 68

Remember when you were a child and went to birthday parties playing this game at the table while enjoying ice cream and cake? There was always uproarious laughter when the message came back to the one who started it. The message that went out was never the one that came back. There were always changes and embellishments. Everyone put their spin on the message, and the results were hilarious.

In this day and age of so many sources of information, it would seem the news we hear is going around a table of children, with each one adding what he or she thinks they hear. So, what is the correct information? What is gospel and what is not? How do we ferret out the real news? What can we believe, and what is someone's idea of what the news really is?

I, for one, go to several sources for the same information and compare. From that I can usually figure out what the real story is. Sometimes it's done for us, like the recent story of the teacher who supposedly duct taped a boy to a chair. Before the real story came out, the medium of restraint changed at least four times in the media. The actual story was that he was taped with a single strand of Scotch tape as a joke. No doubt there will always be some people in this world who think Americans are really duct taping their students to chairs in our schools.

In looking for stories to write, I sometimes go to the newspapers for ideas. I thought I had a great idea for a story when I read in an Eastern Washington paper about a farmer who was building a fence and found a dead baby wrapped in a blue blanket. In my mind's eye, I could see that farmer going across the field with his tractor and post-hole digger, digging holes for the posts and finding the baby by possibly bringing up parts of the blue blanket with his equipment. Chances of finding the baby this way in an open field would be astronomical. I checked with the police department in that area and found the real story was not at all what I imagined. The fact he was building a fence had nothing to do with it. He was merely walking down the road, saw a little bit of blue blanket sticking out of the dirt along the road, decided to investigate, and found the baby.*

Be careful about any news you pass on. America is getting enough bad press. If you do share a story, be sure it is the real one.

*Investigation showed the baby boy died of natural causes. The parents were never found.

Jun 06, 2013

Donald and Daisy

Chapter 69

Our friends from church told us our family needed more pets. We had a dog and cat and thought that was enough. "Oh no," they said. "What you need is a pair of ducks." It never occurred to us that our kids should have ducks for pets or for any other reason. So, we let these friends talk us into it, Donald and Daisy were delivered, and our education about ducks began. You know that old saying that rainy weather is only good for ducks? Not true. Ducks don't like the rain either. When it rained, we knew just where they'd be, on the back porch. That's where they stayed, only to venture out when the rain stopped. I guess you know that made for a lot of cleaning of the back porch.

One thing about ducks, you don't have to invest in slug bait. They are the best when it comes to eliminating slugs. It didn't take long to have a slug-free yard. It also wasn't long before Daisy started nesting, and a new generation of ducks was with us. Of course, occasionally something would get one of the ducklings. We assumed a weasel got it, but we didn't know. No autopsy was done, and we never saw a weasel, either. In fact, we had no clue to what one looked like.

Dick bought one of those half barrels to make a pond for the ducks. He dug a big hole in the terrace where I'd been planting roses. Setting it in the hole, he filled it with water.

The ducks now had a pond and were supposed to stay there. They visited the spot occasionally, but didn't consider it home. The world was their oyster. They traveled. It wasn't long before we began to get phone calls. "Your ducks are here. Come and get them." So, we rounded them up and brought them home.

Daisy nested again and had more little ones. The total was now seventeen ducks. We had to do something. You're probably thinking, why not a duck dinner? Oh, no, not that! You can't eat pets. So that adds a complication. With lots of prayer and the phone book, I started in. Let me tell you, it's really hard to get rid of seventeen ducks all at once, but the Briscoe School for Boys had the answer. They would take all seventeen ducks because they had a pond on their property and other ducks, so ours would be at home there. The next Saturday, we caught all the ducks and put them in boxes to transport in the utility trailer to the school. As we drove up, heads appeared at all the upstairs windows. It seems the boys always checked out company. Boys are curious the world over.

The headmaster, or whoever he was, came out to supervise the process. The ducks were unloaded and taken to the pond, and we left thinking, well, we got rid of that problem, and heaved a sigh of relief. But as usual, it wasn't over yet. Daisy, Donald, and their brood were gone, but we still got calls from neighbors saying, "Your ducks are here. Come and get them." We had to explain they couldn't be our ducks. Our ducks were now at home in Orillia with the boys at Briscoe School. It took awhile, but eventually the calls stopped coming.

Jun 13, 2013

Privacy...What's That?

Chapter 70

What privacy do we have? To save a few bucks on sale items, we sign up for a company's plan and then they have us. Now they can keep track of everything we buy. They know our habits and our whims.

When Safeway first came out with this plan (probably thirty years ago), I didn't like the idea and wouldn't sign up. They have you over a barrel. Either you sign up, or you can't get the sale prices. At that time, people checked the sale papers and went to the stores that had the best prices on what they needed. In fact, people went to several stores to buy only their sale items. I can see why the stores went to this way of dealing with customers. Make them sign up to save money on sale items, and then you have them in the store to buy other items at inflated prices, and the company gains in the long run.

To this day, I do not join these reward systems or clubs. Some of the employees think I'm crazy because I don't join. These stores that require joining their club to get the saving on sale items, become just pick-up stores to me. I go there only to save time (or gas). For real savings, I go to Costco and Winco. Right away you're thinking, you have to sign up and pay to buy at Costco. Well, my husband and I were given a card by our son and then one by our daughter. I continue paying for these cards, because I have found that buying in bulk saves money, time, and gas. Last November I went to Costco and bought facial tissue, paper towels, and toilet paper, telling the checker I'd see him next spring. No matter how bad the weather got or how many colds I got, I didn't have to go to the store for a box of tissues or any other paper item.

To get back to the privacy issue, I've been told that there is a picture of our house on the Internet. It is so good, they say, that if there is a car in the driveway, you can even read the license number. Then there are those listening devices they have advertised, which can pick up what people are saying some distance away. Apparently, someone could be standing in the street in front of your house and listen to what you are saying inside. So much for technology and privacy.

Jun 20, 2013

It's All About Dirt

Chapter 71

When I bought a new clothes dryer a few years ago, I didn't realize that this wonderful machine, that does so many things, was going to make such a change in my life. It was great to have something that would fluff up pillows and other things that needed fluffing and would also take the wrinkles out of clothes that had been hanging in the closet too long. No longer did I have to get out the ironing board. Just a few minutes on Tumble Press, and in no time the wrinkles are gone.

In an old house like mine, when you gain something, you can lose something too. What I lost was my heater in the greenhouse. My son, checking the wiring, said, "Mother, you can't use your new dryer and the heater in the greenhouse. It's one or the other."

Well, there was no contest; the heater had to go. Now, my husband had made the greenhouse by partitioning off one half of the front porch so I could keep my Geraniums there for the winter. He made worktables with shelves, and everything was handy. It was a great job. However, without heat, nothing could be saved in the wintertime. Now the problem has become what to do with dead plants and the dirt they are in.

I thought about that for a while, and one rainy day last month I looked out at the driveway and noticed some puddles out there and decided I needed to fill them up. So, I took those hanging baskets out there put the dead plants in the yard waste container, and dumped the dirt in the puddles.

Well, it's been said you're never too old to learn. This is one lesson I wish I had learned a long time ago. When dirt gets wet, it turns to mud, and when it dries out, it's dirt again (and dust). Dirt gets tracked into the house and other places, and so does mud. Your vacuum cleaner gets full of dirt (and dust that goes through the filter). You not only have to dump the bag, you have to clean up the site where you replace it. Dust flies all over. You also have to take the vacuum cleaner outside and clean it out too. In fact, these things will probably have to be done all summer, unless I get on the ball and order a load of gravel to cover up my big mistake.

Oh, well. Live and learn, I always say.

Jun 27, 2013

The Crash on Long Island Sound

Chapter 72

On July 17, 1996, TWA flight 800 took off from JFK Airport en route to Rome with a stopover in Paris, France. The plane exploded and crashed in Long Island Sound. Of the 230 passengers, none survived.

People involved with finding out the reason for this airplane crash are now coming forward with interesting testimony. They want the investigation reopened and a second look taken. I agree.

These men are retired now and feel that the real cause should be brought out. They said they were told by the FBI, at the time, to say it was brought down by an internal cause, not external, though there was evidence to the contrary.

The night of the crash, I was staying up to finish a project that was needed the next day. Having the television on to keep me company while I worked, news of this crash came on and a reporter showed a film taken by someone at the scene. It was of something going up to the plane, not going the other way. I thought then that it was a missile.

If this was the case, why was there a cover-up? One thought is that those in charge did not want it out that an ordinary missile could bring down a plane. Or was it something else? If it really was a missile, why hide the fact?

The Sunday after these men were on the news with their startling statements, George Stephanopoulus was talking down the idea of a missile on his Sunday program. He said it didn't happen, that there was no need for a new investigation. Is he too quick in coming out against this? What does he know? He was the Senior Advisor for Policy and Strategy in the Clinton Administration before leaving it in December, 1996.

It's going to be interesting to see how this all plays out. A documentary is supposed to air on this subject on July 17, 2013.

Jul 04, 2013

The Way It Used to Be

Chapter 73

When I was volunteering at the museum in Auburn, I came across a picture of a classroom. There was a boy sitting on a stool in the corner next to the blackboard. On his head was a dunce cap. This was not unusual. What was unusual was a rifle leaning against the blackboard. When some people looked at this picture, they assumed that the students were so bad the teacher had the rifle there for order. Others were truly stumped. Finally, a man came into the museum who had actually been in that class. He laughed about the gun being there to keep order. The explanation was simple. He told us it was duck hunting season, and the teacher and students all went duck hunting together after school.

The fact that that gun could be there all the school day says something about those times, too. No child would touch that gun -- not only because it didn't belong to them, but because they were familiar with guns and didn't fool with them. I imagine that all their families had guns and kids would know how to use them. We did at our house. My sisters and I all knew how to shoot. Several times someone would bring a gun to shoot when we were out in the woods for a picnic. A target would be set up next to a hill, and all of us would take a turn at trying to hit the target. There was no mystery about guns, and we never fooled with them.

Boys got Red Ryder BB guns for birthdays, when they were old enough. Then later, probably around sixteen, they would be given a .22 rifle for their birthday. So, guns were always there in case you needed them, especially on a farm. It was the final solution to marauding dogs that attacked and ran the cattle. Once a marauding pack of dogs came in at night and attacked our little dog. He died of his injuries.

Now boys are expelled from school for merely pointing a finger at someone and saying bang! bang! I suppose they can't play cowboys and Indians or cops and robbers any more either. Could this be why kids take up guns and shoot other people, because they are frustrated from not being able to do what boys have done for centuries? It is something to think about.

Jul 11, 2013

Two Kinds of People

Chapter 74

The way I see it, there are only two kinds of people in this world: the builder-uppers and the tear-downers. Many people would take exception to that statement, but living in the same town for over sixty years, I've watched this happen over and over. A group gets together and works on the parks. They gather money and make nice buildings for restrooms, and all is well for a while. Then the vandals take over, and the facilities are destroyed by those they were meant to serve. So, we go from nothing to nice and back to well, Porta-Potties.

People have complained that there are no restrooms that are handicapped accessible. Now the rebuilding must begin all over again. One wonders how long the new buildings will last.

If we could just curtail those tear-downers and help the builder-uppers maintain what they build, things could change. Then maybe we would have good places to take our families to.

It takes people to tell the police what they see. It takes curtailing liquor (and now marijuana) from teenagers, so they won't, in their fuzzy brains, think it's fun to blow up a toilet with an M-80, (or anything else that might not only destroy, but could take a finger or two with it as well.)

The capitol budget for our state was just signed into law by Governor Jay Inslee, and Milton will get $225,000 to "renovate Triangle Park to meet the requirement of the federal Americans with Disabilities Act. This money will go to upgrade the bathrooms, which did not meet the federal standards and as a result have been closed to all members of the public for several years."*

We'll see how long they last this time. If people will let the police know when they see something happening, the buildings might last quite a while. Years ago, when I asked why some of the neighbors hadn't called the police when they heard the noise of things being destroyed, they just said, "Oh, there's something happening over there all the time." So they ignored it.

For those that say and do nothing, when they know something is happening, I say they put themselves in the tear-downers category.

*Milton Edgewood Signal 7-12-13

Jul 18, 2013

Robo and Other Calls

Chapter 75

Robo calls have changed me. I used to be nice to people on the phone. That changed when my husband had his first stroke. In taking care of him, I was besieged with calls, not only from those that would sell me something, but even neighbors who thought now we'd have to sell and they wanted to buy a part of our property.

I realized that by talking to so many of these people, I was losing time to help my husband. So, I began to hang up on them. I no longer would take the time to listen to any of them. They were stealing my time, and I decided I was not going to let them do it anymore. As soon as I find out it's not a family member or a friend, the receiver goes back on the hook, and I go back to what I was doing. At first, I felt a little guilty (only a little), but after that I found satisfaction in thwarting them.

One thing about those robo calls, sometimes their spiel starts before I pick up, so I don't get the first word or words. For example, this morning I picked up the receiver and heard, "Congratulations!" Then the person went on with, "Are you over sixty? Do you live alone?" As I hung up I thought, I am over sixty, and I do live alone, and it's nothing to be congratulated for. So, now I wonder what the "catch" was. No doubt the call will come again and maybe I'll hear enough to find out before I cut them off.

The Rachel calls have gone away, apparently. I haven't gotten any of those for a long time. What I am getting now are, "This is John, from the shipping department," and also the ones that say, "We are giving away security systems in your area."

The people I really hate to hang up on are the ones who are calling for the non-profit groups. However, I have a limited amount of income and very little to give. I decide where that goes at the first of the month. So, I console myself with it's a waste of time for both of us, so hanging up on them cuts their loss of time to a minimum.

So, let me say, if you call me, never start the conversation with, "How are you today?" That's how many of these people start their calls. So, I guess you know this will not get a verbal answer, but that bang of the receiver will tell it all.

Jul 25, 2013

It Was a Weird Week

Chapter 76

It started out with a visit from a neighbor who wanted to know if I knew someone who changed locks. I didn't, but I knew who to ask and got a name and number from her. Since my neighbor does not speak very good English, she had me call and make arrangements. At 10:00 the next day the neighbor came to tell me they had called and were coming at 11:00, which I already knew. I went to her house to help her if she had trouble telling him what she wanted done. They communicated just fine. He reconfigured the locks, took her old keys, and gave her new ones. I thought, now she will have some peace.

The next day she was back at my door saying someone had been in her house again. I talked her into letting me call the police, and soon Officer Williams was at my door. He came in, and we all sat down at the kitchen table and talked about her situation, trying to convince her that since she had the locks changed, no one could get in. Thinking we had her convinced, he left. She went home but was back the next day saying they had come in her house and left some papers. The papers were just instructions for using her appliances. Now it was time for more talking. If she was worried about family members coming to take her things, she should tell her lawyer to send a letter denying them access.

She must be convinced. She hasn't come back. Calling her yesterday, she did make reference to lawyers and laughed, so she seems to be doing all right.

On Friday, I was watching television when the power went out and back on three times. I turned off the television and called Louise, my next-door neighbor, to see if they had the same trouble. She said she didn't see the lights flash and asked her husband and he said, no, he hadn't seen any flashes either. So, I assumed that it was in my system and went outside and checked the fuse box. One looked suspicious, so I put in a new one and went back in the house to watch TV again. My copying machine had turned on by itself, I noticed, so I turned it off and unplugged it.

It was after 9:00 when the phone rang. It was my neighbor. She was laughing. They both had fallen asleep watching TV when my call woke them up. That's when they found out their TV wasn't working and they had to call their son to fix it. He called Direct TV, and they told him a lightning strike or electrical surge had caused it (or maybe the transmission lines in Fife got a hit). Anyway, I was happy to hear it wasn't in my system, and I could now go to bed worry free.

On Sunday night, I was watching 60 Minutes, and during a commercial I decided to fix myself a snack. As I was returning to the living room, I looked out a window and saw a red car in my driveway with the rear door up and a man standing there. I went out to see why he was there. The young man said he had run out of gas. I got his name and he said he lived on 11th Street and was trying to get a relative to bring him some gas, but then he gets a skate board out of the back of his car and says he's going to go after gas. Now it was time to call for back-up. Shortly, a policeman came. He parked on the street. I told him what the guy told me, and he called in the license number. He then knew who the car belonged to and told me he would go to the man's house and tell him either he moved the car or it would be towed. It wasn't long before a girl was sitting on the back of the car, so I went out to talk to her. She kept saying he was coming soon with the gas, and finally he did with a gallon of gas and his skateboard. After pouring it in, he tried to start it. It took several tries and it wasn't working so I went in the house to call a friend with a winch on his truck who could tow them home. I hadn't any more than dialed, when they were knocking on my door to tell me they got it started and to make sure I hadn't called the tow truck. They thanked me profusely for letting them park in my driveway and then left before their gas ran out.

I've heard that things like this go in threes, so this next week should be a quiet one.

Aug 01, 2013

Looking for Clues

Chapter 77

In reading Saturday's paper about cold cases detectives were working on, I remembered something that might be a help to one of their cases. So, I called the number for Detective Gene Miller and left a message. Today he called me. He is working on the murders of two girls that were killed in North End Parks in 1986. Jennifer Bastian was killed in Point Defiance Park, and Michella Welch was killed in Puget Park. Profilers think the person who did this probably had mental issues along with other problems.

What I remembered and told Detective Miller did not help, because the incident occurred a few years earlier. This was what I thought might be a help to them in their search for the perpetrator.

My stepmother and her relatives always met at a picnic on the first Saturday in August. Everybody knew to save that date. All met at the same kitchen area in Point Defiance Park. My husband and I would go early to establish our spot. We got there and, not seeing any cars parked on the road, we took our boxes and baskets and went downhill to the covered kitchen. However, someone was already there. He had started a fire in the big stove and was warming his hands.

At first, we didn't know what to do. It never occurred to us that he might be alone. We just assumed he had come early, like we had, to save the space for others. In talking to him, he seemed like a nice person, and he encouraged us to put any hot dishes we had on the stove to keep them warm. So, then we asked him if others were coming, and he said no. My husband told him that several more people in our group were coming, and if he didn't mind, we'd set the tables for them. He said no, he didn't mind, so we were okay. We had our space. My husband invited him to stay and eat with us, telling him we always had plenty of food, and he said yes.

When everyone got there, we included him with the group as though he was just another relative. After our meal, we all sat at the tables visiting back and forth when the subject of the Mount St. Helens eruption came up, to which this man told all those within hearing, "You know, if they had just put sand on it, that would have stopped it." There was a lot of turning of heads as people tried to figure out which side of the family he was from. My husband and I didn't say anything, but we were awfully glad when this character decided to move on.

Aug 08, 2013

Ken Griffey, Jr.

Chapter 78

Along with the negative publicity about other baseball greats, it was good to read about Ken Griffey, Jr. All he wanted to do was play baseball because he liked to play. He just did his best, and it got him to the Mariner's Hall of Fame (and will probably get him to the National Hall of Fame as well).

When I first heard about Ken Griffey, Jr., I had no clue as to who he was. At the time, I was on a ride-a-long with the Renton Police. My husband and I won this in a silent auction put on by the Renton Civic Theatre.

For this ride, I was passed from one officer to another, I suppose so that I would get a good picture of all the areas in the city. It was a quiet night, and not much was happening. There was a standoff between two factions at an apartment complex where I had to stay in the car, and that ended peaceably. The only other incident was when a woman's car stalled at a light and the officer pushed her car out of the way to a safe place to wait for a tow truck.

Then I got in the car with this young man who was all excited about showing me Ken Griffey, Jr.'s house. This must be someone important, I thought, so I said sure, I'd like to see it. We cruised over into that area and up a slight incline and then he stopped. I assumed the big house with columns and porch lights lit was THE house.

After that, he suggested going to the cemetery and seeing Jimi Hendrix's grave. At the time, I didn't know Jimi Hendrix, either. I declined on that one. Wandering through a cemetery at night, even with a policeman, was not something I cared to do.

The last officer I rode with was going to stop for breakfast. He had no money with him but planned to stop at a cash machine. Wouldn't you know it -- for some reason, they weren't working. We hadn't had cash machines for very long, and occasionally there would be a malfunction. I told him I had money and would be glad to pay for his breakfast, but of course he could not accept. He finally stopped at a Safeway store, bought a package of gum, and cashed a check, and we headed for breakfast. Then I was taken back to the station and the ride was over. Lots of fun to ride and talk to these guys, and now that I know about Ken Griffey, Jr., I see why this young officer was so excited about taking me to see his house.

Aug 15, 2013

The Other Side of Technology

Chapter 79

While we can do all these wonderful things with what has been discovered or invented, we have to put up with the down side. Because we can do things so much faster, errors are compounded, and probably it is not possible to correct them. Not only that, but these things are used against us.

When Major Oliver Conrad, retired, put the name of his real estate company between our two names in the phone book, it forever made a connection, for me, with real estate. Just yesterday, I received a brochure advertising a farm being auctioned in Ellensburg. 459 prime acres are being auctioned off in parcels. I called their 800 number, and a very sympathetic lady said she would take my name off their list. One down and umpteen to go, an impossible task. At least being mistaken for a real estate agent is not bad when I think of people who get their names mixed up in something criminal and can't get rid of it. Now, that's scary.

The phones are also being used to scam people. I've told the nurses at my doctor's office, don't start your conversation with me by saying, "How are you today," because I'll hang up on you. That's the way many scammers start their conversations. So those who can legitimately ask, can't.

Then there's the mail. Because of technology, the printed word is spread. Lists are passed out. My name is on so many lists and is spreading to other lists all the time. The only good thing about that is I never find an empty mailbox. If there is nothing in my box, I call the Post Office to find out what happened. They get right on it. They know there's something wrong, because I always get mail.

One final thought: be careful who you send money to, especially with a check. Your name, address, and phone number are on that check. I am now trying to get rid of the American Bible Society. After sending them a $10.00 check for bibles to give to military personnel, I have gotten several letters, phone calls, and now a magazine. I may not be able to get off their list but they are definitely off mine!

Aug 22, 2013

School Days
Are Here Again

Chapter 80

The kids will be getting a fairly good education, while their moms take a breather. They will be able to be children and laugh and play with their friends, and learn, too. It was not always so.

In reading the biography of Ralph Waldo Emerson, born May 25, 1803, I find that people who wanted their children to become ministers of the gospel, lawyers, doctors, or others of a learned category were put in the infant school to start with. "Babies of less than three years sat in stiff little rows presided over by sad-faced widows or old maids who kept the switch handy, rebuking even a smile during class hours, and those hours were long." (Hildegarde Hawthorne)

These children went from Infant School to Grammar School, then to Latin School, and when the boys were thirteen or fourteen, they were ready to go to college. School was year-round. There was no time to play. They lost their childhood. By seventeen or eighteen, they were working as teachers to earn money to go on with their schooling or to help with the education of other family members.

What a world that must have been. I loved to see my children laughing and playing. I can't imagine standing over a child, making them learn not only their letters, but prayers, texts, and Bible verses before the age of three. For my children, doing their homework was always important. They had to do that first, before they could play. However, I hope their lives were balanced between work and play. That was something we didn't think about. What we did think about was including as many things as we could that were interesting. Things they would learn from or had a chance to do.

Taking them to Moats Berry Farm to pick berries was one of the things they got to do. It was a chance for them to learn about earning money. Some of the kids that picked berries there had to earn money to buy their school clothes. Whatever our kids earned, they could spend any way they wanted.

In this day and age, we have to worry about security. Our hope and prayers are for safety for the children so they can both work at their studies and have fun as well.

Aug 29, 2013

Show and Tell

Chapter 81

Kids in kindergarten get to show and tell. Many funny things come out of this segment of their learning. It's surprising how vocal kids can get when they have the class's attention. Some say very little, where others expound at length, leaving nothing to others' imaginations.

Now the world has a great big show and tell in Facebook and others of this type. So much is shared with anyone who cares to look at it. Then the best, that is the best some producer decides, is shared on Right This Minute (and I suppose there are other programs that do the same thing on other channels).

I wonder how long it will be before this trend will become "old hat." The innocence of children will be exploited to the point where no one is interested in what children say and do anymore, and something else will have to be found to satisfy the public appetite.

Some of the things said in kindergarten class when I was a secretary in the Enumclaw Grade School back in the forties wouldn't upset anyone now because of what has become the "norm."

One statement a little girl made in show and tell was whispered around among the teachers because it was so scandalous. She told her class, "My big sister is sleeping with another boyfriend. Mama hopes she marries this one."

Different times, different attitudes, different ways of expressing things. The only thing we can be positive about the future is that we are sure to find things to laugh about.

Sep 05, 2013

The Quarter

Chapter 82

Truck drivers lead a different kind of life than the rest of us. It's sometimes exciting and sometimes boring. Some drivers run the same route every day. Others have jobs with different destinations all the time. Some haul the same type of cargo, and others haul different things. We depend on them all.

One man, Chuck Carolan, told me he once drove truck for a German farmer who grew sugar beets. This farmer wanted him to drive that truck to the processing plant as fast as he could to deliver as many loads in a day as possible. Chuck said the farmer told him, "I want to see sugar beets on the ground at every curve all the way to town." (If sugar beets were coming off the truck on every curve, that would show the farmer that he was really traveling fast.)

My father, Allyn O'Neill, drove a cement truck at one time. That is, he hauled dry cement from Seattle to Des Moines. That dry cement was then mixed and, when ready, filled the regular cement mixers. Those trucks would then deliver the cement to the job sites.

My father was also told to go as fast as he could. His boss added that he would pay all traffic fines. You can imagine that there was quite a shuffle at the dry cement plant. Since these trucks carried something that kept other plants going, they always had to rush. If you could get ahead of someone in line, well, guys did it. When there is so much competition, there is trouble. It wasn't long before my father had to have it out with a guy who kept taking advantage of him. The man made the mistake of taking a swing at my father in an argument. My father, who had milked cows for many years, had big, big hands, and even though he was smaller than this man, he packed a harder wallop and knocked the man down with the first blow. That showed that man and others that Father was not to be messed with.

The other side of this job was looking for things to mitigate the boring. There were many traffic lights between Seattle and Des Moines. One day, my father saw a quarter lying on the blacktop while he was waiting for a red light to change. After that, every time he stopped for a red light at that intersection, he looked for the quarter. Each time he could see that it sank a little more into the blacktop, until the last time, when it disappeared altogether.

Sep 12, 2013

Service Dogs

Chapter 83

When my friend, Joann Lakin, told me she took her Irish Wolfhound to the Veterans Hospital as a service dog, it made me wonder about this. Do dogs really help? The Irish Wolfhounds are so big they can get their heads close to the patient and make it easy for a wounded person to touch the dog. I wondered about this therapy but never expected to see it or partake in it.

However, two weeks ago, I was feeling so rotten I decided to go to the emergency room. While sitting in the waiting room with my daughter Anna Marie, a woman came in with a black Lab on a leash. He had a harness on, but she carried the vest she wanted him to wear. This dog had a bit of an attitude. She said he refused to work with the vest on. They compromised, and she carried it. He was a beautiful dog and friendly enough. He sat on my foot while the three of us talked. There was a little boy in the waiting room, probably about three years old, who was really taken by the dog. He would have led that dog all around the room if he'd had the chance. Some people were not willing to touch the dog, and it was obvious that others could hardly wait until the dog came to them.

I was admitted to a room on the third floor and was surprised to have a woman come through on that floor with her black German Shepherd. My family has had more than one German Shepherd, and we find them to be highly intelligent and so loving, and this dog was definitely the same. Because he was larger, I was able to pet Jasper from my bed. He was one of the kind of dogs that you can bond with right away. The handler, Susan, gave us a card telling all about Jasper. This German Shepherd has his own web site. When I got home, I checked it out. Sure enough, he has a web site and it says he has been a part of Pet Partners since 9-11. (His web site address is http://bit.ly/NSSamh)

His life is chronicled on this web site. It tells you what he likes to do and what his favorite treat is, etc. This web site is also a place to donate to FirstGiving. So far, they have collected a whole $25.00. Hopefully for their sake, that improves.

It was a surprise to see both dogs in a hospital, and I think they must help, or they wouldn't be allowed. Just talking to the handlers is a plus. They are good people with the best motives. They and their dogs take you away from what bothers you at the moment and give you a different perspective about your situation. On the negative side, I hear that people are passing off their own dogs as service dogs and causing trouble in grocery stores and other places they take them. I hope they don't spoil this for those that have been taking their time and energy to really make things better for others.

Sep 26, 2013

Closing the Door

Chapter 84

Now you would think that closing a door would be ingrained in everyone. When our kids were little, we were always reminding them to close the back door during the winter, and in the summer it was the opposite, until they got it right. So, then later they would ask, "Do you want the door open or shut?" They learned to give people a choice. By then they knew the importance of the door to the comfort of the people who lived there.

It was a surprise to me when I had to ask one of the medics who responded to my 911 call on Monday to close the door. Of course, these guys are in their heavy clothes and don't feel the cold and are only concentrating on the patient. They did a very good job of taking care of me and getting me to the hospital. In doing so, they got me out of the house, out of the yard, and out the driveway to their vehicle. All was well, and soon we were on our way to St Francis in Federal Way to check out my problem of dizziness.

What they didn't do was shut the back door. They had already fixed the screen door so it would stay open, and so there was the house open to all comers, whether they were two- or four-legged, not to mention winged creatures. There was also the loss of heat to consider.

The house remained that way until my neighbor, who doesn't speak English very well, decided to come down and see how I was after tests I'd had at Virginia Mason Hospital last Friday. When she found the house this way, she panicked. Not having a cell phone to call 911, and picturing me hurt somewhere in the house, she went in thinking to rescue me. But I wasn't there. Then she was really in a panic. She shut the door and rushed over to her next-door neighbor's and found out I'd been taken away in an ambulance

I was checked out, found that I had Positional Vertigo plus too much Warfarin and told I could go home. Anna Marie and I knew the door would be unlocked, because I had the only key with me (that will change), but it was a surprise to us when we found out that the door was left open and grateful to my friend and neighbor, Ida, for closing it. I think I'll have a sign made that says DON'T FORGET TO SHUT THE DOOR prominently placed.

Oct 03, 2013

How to Make a Cake in Ten Minutes

Chapter 85

Have you used your microwave oven to its fullest? Have you experimented with the possibilities of what it can do? If not, I have something for you to try: a chocolate cake made in ten minutes from start to finish. Of course, there are differences in microwaves so you might have to experiment a bit to find out how yours works. Always remember you DO NOT use any kind of metal in a microwave oven. (That includes foil wrap. My husband found out that was a no-no when he tried to pop popcorn still in its plastic and foil bag. It necessitated buying a new Microwave.)

Recipe for Chocolate Microwave Cake:

1 egg	2 tsps. baking powder
3 tbsps. oil	1 C flour
¼ C cocoa	2/3 C Milk
½ C sugar	

Beat egg and oil. Add cocoa and sugar. Mix well. Add flour and milk mixing well. Beat until smooth. Grease a baking dish, preferably a 7" or 8" square casserole dish. Bake in microwave oven for four minutes at 7 power.

When done, remove from oven with potholders and drop some chocolate chips over the top. Cover with a dishtowel and leave for a couple of minutes. Remove towel and spread the now melted chocolate over the top of the cake. It is then ready to serve.

My guys that take care of the yard have all put their stamp of approval on this cake. They always come back for more.

Oct 10, 2013

Sears Bargain Basement

Chapter 86

My husband and I spent many happy hours in that basement. My sister, who lived in Eastern Washington (a four hour drive away), told us about it. In telling us, she mentioned all the bargains in kids' clothes you could find there. I was eager to take off right away to see what I could find for our three girls and one boy. My husband, not so much, but I managed to talk him into it. Once we got there and he found tools and other guy things, I never had to twist his arm again.

At first, I hesitated in digging into piles of clothing in order to find the sizes we needed. It wasn't long before I got over that and was not only finding sizes for my family, but also looking for sizes others were shopping for. We were sort of united in our efforts to clothe our families for school.

After the clothes, we looked around to see what else was offered. When our son wanted a baseball mitt, we were happy to find a great big pile of mitts, all for the wrong hand. My husband persisted and went through that whole pile and finally found one that was for a right-handed person.

They eventually closed the bargain basement. They must have realized that many of us went to the basement store first. Then if we didn't find what we wanted, we went upstairs and paid regular prices for things. While the basement store was still open, we bought a washer and dryer for much less than the upstairs price and hauled it home. Also bought an oil stove for our kitchen. This was an important find. It was made to go next to a cooking stove, so it was white enameled on one side and black metal on the side that went next to our electric stove. It was the only one they had, and it was perfect for us. I am using it even today.

I did have one problem. I was there by myself and bought a drapery rod for our front room windows, never thinking about how I was going to get it in the car. The guys that were sitting on the steps taking their break figured that out right away and kept making comments and laughing. All that did was make me mad, and I would have gotten that rod in the car if I had to bend it double. The top of the cardboard container broke off and fell on the ground. I ignored it; pushing the long box into the car, I shut the door. It wasn't until I got home that I found I only had one end piece for the rod. The other must have been in the cardboard that broke off in the parking lot. No matter, I just put the end piece in the Goodwill bag and used the rod the way it was. In 20 years, nobody has noticed.

Oct 17, 2013

Yeti and Sasquatch

Chapter 87

A British scientist, Bryan Sykes, thinks he has solved the mystery of the Abominable Snowman. He thinks it is a bear. "It may be a hybrid between polar bears and brown bears." He also states, "Finding a living creature could explain whether differences in appearance and behavior to other bears account for descriptions of the Yeti as a hairy hominid."

It is my opinion that the same thing could be true with our Sasquatch. The reason I am so interested in this is because I saw something years ago that has had me wondering ever since. In 1951, when our oldest daughter, Anna Marie, was two months old, my father and I rode horses to the top of Huckleberry Mountain in the Cascades to pick huckleberries. While there, the horses became really nervous and jumpy. I thought it was because horse flies were bothering them. Soon my father called me over to the edge of the cliff to see what was bothering the horses. A huge animal, light gray in color, was walking across the plateau below. The horses could smell it, but the animal could not smell the horses because the wind drafts were blowing in our direction. He (or she) was walking upright and swinging his arms through the huckleberry bushes as he passed through, bringing the berries and leaves up to his mouth, and we could see the leaves fluttering back to the ground. In the middle of this plateau was a Forest Service outhouse. These are probably 7 feet tall, and you could see as this animal passed by it that he was taller than the building. Standing straight, he walked on two feet, like a man, all the way across this big expanse and went off into the woods, still walking on two legs.

Afterwards, my father said bear, I said Sasquatch. We argued for a few years over it, but I finally realized Father was right. It was probably a grizzly bear. Seeing a huge animal standing upright and walking like a human being could certainly fuel a myth.

Oct 24, 2013

Weird Things That Happen in an Old House

Chapter 88

The children and I were sitting in the living room talking. Their father, my husband, was in the hospital recovering from surgery, so he was not there to protect us. All of a sudden, we heard footsteps upstairs. What to do? I was sure there was no one up there, and then I thought if we don't go up there and check it out, no one will be able to sleep up there. So, I gathered up the kids and we marched up the stairs. We looked into the bathroom, checked the bathtub and behind the door. Then we went on down the hall to the hall closet and checked it out. No one was there. We checked under the beds in both bedrooms, the closets, and behind doors, and found nothing. The kids were satisfied, but I still wondered.

It was fall, and I was down in the cellar rearranging my jars on the shelves opposite the stairs. All of a sudden, I saw shadows moving and turned quickly to see if someone was coming down the stairs behind me, but no one was there. I turned back to look at the concrete where I'd seen the shadows, and there they were, still moving. Looking more intensely, the shadows looked like clouds. They looked like what I see when I'm outside and look up the hill in back of our house. The cloud movements are usually the same, going from right to left. Somehow the scene was being transferred from outside to the wall in the cellar. Was it a tiny hole in the foundation with a drop of water as a lens? Or what?

Then there was a funeral notice in the paper about a Mr. Amidon who died at the age of 76. Amidons had lived in our house some time ago, and I decided if this Mr. Amidon had lived here, he would have been a child. A couple of days after I read his obituary, my husband and I were sitting in our recliner chairs watching TV. All of a sudden, we heard footsteps on the front porch. As no one ever comes to the front porch, we thought one of our kids was coming that way to surprise us (or something). It was then that the front door, which always sticks, swung open with a bang, and no one was there. Being the closest to the door, I got up to close it, telling my husband, "Mr. Amidon has come home."

Oct 31, 2013

Living by an Intersection

Chapter 89

Through the years, many, many cars, motorcycles, bicycles, and pedestrians have gone through the cross streets I live by and had no trouble. Occasionally, by fate or what have you, two will come together and sadness ensues. Last week I was taking a nap and when I woke up decided to go outside. Stepping off the porch, I heard the shouting of angry words and noticed a car by my front gate. There was another car parked a ways behind it. A woman was rushing back and forth hollering, among other things.

"My husband will kill me!" It was obviously only a fender bender. Not being able to keep quiet, I hollered at her to calm down. Twice I hollered adding, "It's only a fender bender." She did settle down then and began looking at the damage. My next thought was to call 911. Thankfully, I came to my senses and went back in the house. People have cell phones and they are adults. They can take care of this themselves. About the husband killing her, I really doubt it would come to that. However, I remember when I was working for the Fife School District and a woman I worked with went shopping on her lunch hour and came back not only late, but also quite upset. She'd been in an accident and called her husband for support and was very unhappy because he wanted to know how bad the car was damaged, not asking her first if she was hurt. It could kill a marriage.

When I noticed the people were gone, I decided to drive down and get my mail. Just getting out on the road, I saw two police cars, one blocking the intersection and another one that had come up the hill stopped at the stop sign on the street I was on. The young man, with a friend, was standing in the road talking to the officer in the intersection. Oh, what to do? Is this a crime scene, or what? This could be ticket time if I wasn't careful. I signaled for a right turn. After a bit, the officer in the intersection slowly moved forward. I made my turn nodding and smiling at the two young men on my left, as I drove around the police car. Never even looking at the officer, I proceeded to my mailbox. Not having guts to go back the way I came, I went around the four blocks to get home.

Nov 07, 2013

Anyone for Apples?

Chapter 90

Realizing my life had changed when my husband passed away, I had to take stock and decide how I would live my life from here on out. Living in a hundred-year-old house with an orchard and pasture decided me. What I have is a mini-farm. Therefore, it was time to work with it and do what I could. Money wasn't an issue. Though I have very little, I have enough to get by.

So, what to do? Sheep we already had. They eat the grass and any blackberry plants that try to gain entry. Their wool was already going to Fort Nisqually to be used for demonstrations. So that would continue as long as our neighbor's granddaughter, Kimberly Rose, would take it to them. That left the orchard. At that time, the apples were full of worms and the apple maggot had presented itself. Bob Johnson, my yard maintenance guy, told me about a spraying company that took care of his mom's orchard, and I called them. That's all it took. With care, there soon were good apples that people wanted. All I had to do was fill up boxes and put them out by the road with a "Free" sign, and the apples would be taken by those who wanted them.

Even so, this year being such a good year for apples, I thought I would have to dump a lot in the garbage. But that has not happened. My next-door neighbor, who has a juicer, came and got some boxes of apples to make juice. He came back on the weekend to pick up all that my yard guy had put into 8 or 10 garbage sacks, and he took those to his church, and they were made into cider.

After another storm, the ground was littered with mostly green apples that really weren't ready to be used. Bob picked up all of these. Put them in sacks on the chairs in the patio. Some went in a bucket, and he even put some in an empty planter. A few were ripe enough to use, and those were put out to the road and were taken by someone. The rest I thought would surely go in the yard waste container. But no, I met a friend at the Post Office who had given me hay that her goats didn't like. Maybe the goats would like some apples. She told me she assumed her goats would like some apples, but she knew her 150 chickens would for sure. So, she came and took away all the sacks, boxes, and apples she could. Bob tells me there are still apples on that last tree, so we are not done yet, but the end is in sight. Hopefully, none will have to go in the garbage.

Nov 14, 2013

Money in the Mail

Chapter 91

Do you open all your mail? I do and once in a while I find money. It comes in pennies, nickels, dimes, and quarters. Once an appeal for money included a dollar bill. I thought they would take my name off their list when they didn't get a reply. However, this went on for seven years. My lawyer friend, who was an intelligence officer in the Vietnam War, dropped leaflets from planes, and when they got any kind of response, they knew they were on target. So, he told me not to answer these things. So, I don't do anything with appeals I'm not familiar with. I did buy a ceramic piggy bank and put it in the kitchen window. All these coins that come in are dropped in that bank. Earlier in the year, I opened it and counted $3.32. Just lately, I picked it up and it was heavy, so I decided it was time to empty it again. There was $3.18. So, now I had collected $6.50. Getting out my last grocery receipt from Albertsons, I looked to see what I had bought that would come close to this amount. There was a box of Kellogg's Raisin Bran for $4.99 and bananas for $1.47. That would have taken the $6.50, leaving me with four cents in change and taken care of breakfast for a week or more.

There are all kinds of things beside money that come in the mail: book marks, notepads, ink pens, greeting cards of all kinds, wrapping paper, and calendars. Our church collects calendars for Kiros (a prison ministry). I've given them seven already and have three more to deliver. To get so many, my name is probably on several lists and spreading to more. It's nice that we have recycling. At least all that paper doesn't go to waste but is made into something else which, in the long run, saves trees, I hope.

Nov 21, 2013

The Green Bean
Casserole

Chapter 92

It's now official. The green bean casserole is a part of our holiday fare. Shari's is now advertising it as one of the side dishes you can get with their holiday feast. It is included along with the stuffing, turkey gravy, mashed potatoes, sweet potatoes, and cranberry sauce. They will gladly have it ready for you to pick up and take home. Their ad was in my mailbox today picturing these delightful items and letting us know they will be serving up this feast from Thanksgiving to Christmas. "Just heat, serve and enjoy."

How many years has the green bean casserole been advertised to get us convinced that we should serve this with our holiday meals? There are a variety of thoughts on this. Some say the sixties. I think it was later than that, but I don't know. It seemed like everyone joked about it at first. Then it was ignored, but the advertisers persisted, and finally it has been accepted. There are now displays in the grocery stores with cans of green beans, mushroom soup, and French fried onions. The stores are getting ready for the seasonal rush for the traditional items, and they don't want us to forget this part of it.

I can just see those PR people giving each other high fives because they made it happen. That makes me wonder what is going to follow the green bean casserole. Makes me also wonder how far they can go. I wish these guys or gals would take on world peace. Given enough time, maybe they could make that happen, too.

Nov 28, 2013

Football Games and Background Noise

Chapter 93

Well the Twelfth Man has done it again. They broke the record for noise. I suppose this trend will go on and the Kansas City people will be busting their eardrums to beat us.

Not a fan of football, though I like to see that our local team is winning, what works for me is the noise factor on television. When the house is too quiet, I find it hard to work. Having raised four children, taken care of grandchildren and great grandchildren, I'm used to noise. So, what to do? If I turn the television to a sit-com or a movie, soon I find myself involved in listening and not getting my work done. When I wanted to find one of these programs at a time when I could take a break (especially on Saturdays), all I found were football games. That's when I realized it didn't matter who was playing, how the game was going, who was doing what. It was the roar of the crowd and the announcer's patter that dulled everything for me. So, Saturday was the day to get the most work done.

There was a time when I was interested in football. My son played in high school. I'm sure there are many fine points to the game, and I should have gone to the library and got a book on it. But I was just too busy at the time, so I sat next to my husband and expected him to explain everything to me. He was too engrossed in the game to tell me the important points, so I just yelled when he did. I did know when our team made a touchdown and knew that was good.

There was a time, when I was in the sixth grade, that a neighbor boy wanted to teach my sisters and I to play football, but my father quickly put a stop to that. Girls didn't play football, especially the contact kind.

Now I've found the perfect place for a football game. This background noise of fans roaring and announcers shouting should help me get those personal notes I like to write on my Christmas cards done and in the mail on time. Who would have thought?

Dec 05, 2013

The Much-Maligned Fruitcake

Chapter 94

So much has been said about the dreaded gift of fruitcake. However, there is a woman who is sending a fruitcake to Steve Poole, the weatherman on KOMO-TV. She is certain he will like hers. He joked about maybe people hated fruitcake because they got one that was "re-gifted" so many times that it was hard as a rock.

My experience with fruitcake started some 55 years ago, when a neighbor gave me her recipe for Applesauce Fruitcake. She brought it with her from the Mid-west. It was something that was quite popular where she had grown up, and she thought she should share it, especially with someone who had so many apples. Her original recipe called for lard. I have changed that to a healthier oil. Otherwise, the recipe is the same as she gave me.

This was a great thing for us. I began making the cakes and sending them to all the relatives we had who were in the service. Through the years that fruitcake has gone to England, Germany, South Korea, and many parts of the United States.

Always sending it to my children, I was told what happened when I sent it to my son and his wife when she was in the hospital. He and his buddy were coming off shift at the police department and picked the cake up along with other mail and had the cake half eaten before they got the quarter mile to the house. I guess that's as good a commercial for the cake as I could get.

I once sent a loaf of banana bread and a fruitcake to my nephew Allyn in New York. He was stationed there with the Coast Guard. I am happy to note that he let me know the banana bread was spoiled when it got there, but the fruitcake was fine, and he enjoyed it.

Since this is a seasonal thing, I'll be making a new batch soon to share and maybe change a few minds. That is if they try it.

Dec 12, 2013

You Can't Quarantine Christmas

Chapter 95

When I was in the fifth grade, my oldest sister came down with Scarlet Fever. She stayed home. I went to school. Always talking, it wasn't long before I was telling my teacher about this red rash my sister had on her stomach. She in turn told the principal who in turn told the school nurse.

This ended up in my being advised to gather up all my things and wait in the auditorium for someone to come and get me. Chairs were set up for lunch, and children filed in to sit in them and eat their lunch, but my chair was in the big open space, and no one was supposed to come near. One of my friends did come to find out why I was sitting there with my coat on, but the principal made her go away. So, there I sat, all alone and definitely lonely, being stared at by the whole school (except those who went home for lunch). Probably they wondered what I'd done wrong.

When I got home, there was this red sign nailed to our front door. We were in quarantine. No one could come in, and no one could go out, except the doctor.

My father, who drove a milk truck at the time, could not live in the house and still work. So, he moved into the barn until we got over this problem. It wasn't long before my other sister and I came down with it too. So, Mother set up our beds in the living room where it would be warmer. She also tried, unsuccessfully, to keep our little sister away from us. But the house was too small, and our sister was too young to understand. She just wanted to be where we were. However, she didn't come down with it and neither did Mother.

Christmas Eve came and Mother hung our stockings by the stove. There was no tree. With three beds in the living room, there wasn't room. We awoke the next morning to see our stockings bulging with candy and an orange. It was like any other Christmas, except we hadn't gone to our grandmother's on Christmas Eve with all our aunts, uncles, and cousins. And Father couldn't be with us (though he waved to us every day through the front window). Some relatives sent presents, and so on Christmas morning we listened to Christmas music on the radio and opened our presents. Mother (and Father too) made it a festive occasion for us. There was lots of love as always. And that is what Christmas is made of. It's the reason no quarantine could destroy it.

Dec 19, 2013

More About Christmas

Chapter 96

Yes, no quarantine could take away the love that comes down at Christmas. It's too bad that everyone can't maintain this feeling throughout the year.

It's impossible now for me to remember what presents I got that year except for one. That was the book Black Beauty. My cousin Eleanor sent it to me. It was the greatest gift at that time, and why I remember it so well.

In reading, you can take yourself out of the world you're in and spend time in another one. So that's how we spent our time, reading and, of course, calling out to mother. "She's in here again," and so Mother would come and take Margaret out to the kitchen with her and try to find something for her to color or just try to distract her and keep her away from us sick ones.

The quarantine did not last forever. Only I'm sure at the time it seemed like forever. Soon the nurse came. She checked us out and removed the red sign from the door (leaving only the nails). Then she gave Mother a canister and instructions on how to fumigate the house. After that was done, we could go back to school, and our family could get back to normal. I don't know who was happiest about that. I'm sure it was a toss-up.

That afternoon as Father put more wood in the kitchen stove and then got the car out, Mother got us into our warm clothes and placed the canister on the stove. Then all six of us went for a two-hour ride while the canister fumigated the house. I still wonder how anything could be so powerful that it could fumigate a two-bedroom house from the kitchen stove. My parents may have wondered too. Those were the rules at that time, so they followed them, and we were reunited at last.

And now to get to this Christmas.... We had our traditional Christmas gathering of family and had a wonderful time. I didn't think there was going to be a tree, because I had put it off until the very last day. However, our good friend Bill Rochelle came with his truck and solved the problem by taking me up to Rite Aid, where they had trees left. Not only that, those $29.00 trees were now free. That made me realize procrastinating isn't all that bad, at least at Christmas.

Dec 26, 2013

The Appreciation Jar

Chapter 97

A year ago, Anna Marie and Kirk gave me a Happy Appreciation Jar for Christmas, along with other things. You are to fill it with things that give your life more meaning. It's a place to record those special things that make you glad you're a member of the human race. At the end of the year, you take out these notes, pictures, and any items that made your life more enjoyable and go over them.

I'd forgotten about winning two $35.00 tickets for a crab feed in Puyallup. Even though I didn't go, the tickets reminded me of the night I won them. I bought two tickets to a fundraiser so my friend and I could go to the dinner. At the last minute, she decided she didn't want to go, so I had to go alone. I looked around the room and saw a single seat at a table in the back and asked if it was taken. Immediately I was told to join them, and they treated me as though I was one of their favorite people. For that evening, I was one of their group. They introduced me to everyone and made me feel so at home with them. When it came time to put our ticket stubs in a basket for a drawing, the husband took mine and put it in, even though I said I didn't need to try for a prize. "Oh yes," he said, "You've got to be a part of this." And so, I won the tickets. Even though I wasn't able to use those tickets, they were in the jar to remind me of these wonderful people.

Many reminders were in the jar to show me that regardless of what you hear or see on the news, the world is full of wonderful people.

I couldn't finish this without mentioning the man I encountered at the Post Office one day last summer. I drove up and parked my car. As I got out, I noticed a man coming out the door. When he saw me, he stopped and held the door for me. As I was quite a ways from him, I walked faster so he wouldn't be inconvenienced by waiting for me. He immediately said, "Don't hurry," and so relieved, I did walk at my usual pace. He stayed there holding the door for me. Then he said as I went through, "Have a good day." I don't have a clue who he was, just a middle-aged man with courtesy and a short bit of time to make the day better for me.

Jan 02, 2014

About the Author

For nearly eight decades LaVerna Conrad has dedicated herself to the passionate pursuit of writing. Even before beginning elementary school, she was deeply connected to the written word...whether listening to the local librarians read at story hour while soaking up the sights, sounds and smells of the place, or making her own books and stitching them together with needle and thread. Her earliest memories revolve around writing and reading.

In junior high she had her first chance at editing when her mother, who had left school in 8th grade, asked LaVerna to edit her letters to make sure they were grammatically correct.

Deeply curious and highly observant, LaVerna embraces all life experiences as interactive training opportunities that provide grist for her writing mill. During a police ride-along purchased at a charity auction she found herself sitting in a squad car with the officer guarding a body while waiting for the coroner to come and pick up this man that the EMTs could not resuscitate.

Married for 60 years with four grown children, LaVerna has a varied and diverse work history ranging from making dinner for the neighbors, who were turkey farmers, to being a telephone operator to cataloging and classifying books and materials for the local school district where she learned how to put the essence of a 400 page book on a 3 x 5 card.

If you are looking for help clarifying your ideas, getting your thoughts on paper or learning the craft of writing for publication, get a copy of her *Writing Kit for Beginning Writers* at her website, LaVernaJConrad.com.

Writing is a craft you can do as long as you are able. After all these years LaVerna is still putting pen to paper.